lonely planet

D0293006

HONG KONG
ENCOUNTER

ANDREW STONE

Hong Kong Encounter

Published by Lonely Planet Publications Pty Ltd
ABN 36 005 607 983

Australia	Head Office, Locked Bag 1, Footscray, Vic 3011 ☎ 03 8379 8000 fax 03 8379 8111 talk2us@lonelyplanet.com.au
USA	150 Linden St, Oakland, CA 94607 ☎ 510 250 6400 toll free 800 275 8555 fax 510 893 8572 info@lonelyplanet.com
UK	2nd fl, 186 City Rd London EC1V 2NT ☎ 020 7106 2100 fax 020 7106 2101 go@lonelyplanet.co.uk

The first edition was written by Steve Fallon. This edition was commissioned in Lonely Planet's Melbourne office and produced by: **Commissioning Editors** Rebecca Chau, Emily K Wolman **Coordinating Editors** Kristin Odijk, Martine Power **Coordinating Cartographer** Jacqueline Nguyen **Layout Designer** Paul Iacono **Managing Editor** Katie Lynch **Managing Cartographer** David Connolly **Managing Layout Designer** Laura Jane **Cover Designer** Pepi Bluck **Project Manager** Chris Love **Series Designer** Mik Ruff **Thanks to** Adam Bextream, Yvonne Bischofberger, Melanie Dankel, Bruce Evans, Ryan Evans, Quentin Frayne, Jennifer Garrett, Yvonne Kirk, Lisa Knights, Rebecca Lalor, Glenn van der Knijff, Wayne Murphy, Celia Wood

ISBN 978 1 74104 879 7

Printed by Hang Tai Printing Company, Hong Kong. Printed in China.

Mixed Sources
Product group from well-managed forests and other controlled sources
www.fsc.org Cert no. SGS-COC-005002
© 1996 Forest Stewardship Council

HOW TO USE THIS BOOK
Colour-Coding & Maps
Colour-coding is used for symbols on maps and in the text that they relate to (eg all eating venues on the maps and in the text are given a green knife and fork symbol). Each neighbourhood also gets its own colour, and this is used down the edge of the page and throughout that neighbourhood section.

Prices
Multiple prices listed with reviews (eg $10/5 or $10/5/20) indicate adult/child, adult/concession or adult/child/family.

Send us your feedback We love to hear from readers — your comments help make our books better. We read every word you send us, and we always guarantee that your feedback goes straight to the appropriate authors. The most useful submissions are rewarded with a free book. To send us your updates and find out about Lonely Planet events, newsletters and travel news visit our award-winning website: **lonelyplanet.com/contact**.

Note: We may edit, reproduce and incorporate your comments in Lonely Planet products such as guidebooks, websites and digital products, so let us know if you don't want your comments reproduced or your name acknowledged. For a copy of our privacy policy visit **lonelyplanet.com/privacy**.

ANDREW STONE

In 2000 Andrew quit a sensible job in London in a bid to travel and to make it as a freelance writer. Hong Kong was his first destination, where he spent an unforgettable year and a bit. Home was sleepy Lamma Island, his base for exploring Hong Kong and the wider region. He has returned every year since to research various guidebooks and newspaper articles about this very special city, including the 13th edition of Lonely Planet's *Hong Kong & Macau City Guide*.

ANDREW'S THANKS

My fellow authors on *Hong Kong & Macau City Guide*, Chung Wah and Reggie Ho, helped me out in so many ways (again) on this title with ideas, suggestions and contacts. I am indebted to them. Thanks also to Liz Lam from Macau Tourism for her ready help with my queries and to my commissioning editor Rebecca Chau for her patience and advice throughout.

THE PHOTOGRAPHER

Greg Elms completed a Bachelor of Arts in Photography at the Royal Melbourne Institute of Technology, then embarked on a travel odyssey across Australia, Southeast Asia, India, Africa, Europe and the Middle East. He has been the photographer for numerous award-winning books, and has worked for magazines, ad agencies, designers and, of course, book publishers such as Lonely Planet.

Our readers Many thanks to the travellers who wrote to us with helpful hints, useful advice and interesting anecdotes. Penny Lattey, Ryan Macdicken, Devon Peavoy, Jacalyn Soo, Lois Warner, Rachel Willcocks.

Cover photograph Cityscape across Hong Kong's Victoria Harbour, Thierry Dosogne/Riser/Getty Images. **Internal photographs** p52, p72, p85, p104, p153 by Andrew Stone. All other photographs by Lonely Planet Images, and by Greg Elms except p32 Andrew Burke; p13, p26, p27, p50 Michael Coyne; p47 Krzysztof Dydynski; p28 Alain Evrard; p24 Manfred Gottschalk; p6, p57, p97 John Hay; p6 Tim Hughes; p17, p88, p98, p114, p128, p138 Richard I'Anson; p164 Holger Leue; p66 Oliver Strewe; p31 Dallas Stribley; p8, p32, p160, p173 Phil Weymouth.

All images are copyright of the photographers unless otherwise indicated. Many of the images in this guide are available for licensing from **Lonely Planet Images:** www.lonelyplanetimages.com.

Take in the sights aboard one of Hong Kong's unique double-decker trams (p13)

CONTENTS

THIS IS HONG KONG

A city that forces you to make some rapid adjustments. From the calm and cool of a Kowloon hotel lobby, the heat and hustle of teeming streets engulf you. You fight your way through multitudes only to stumble into sudden shade, greenery and space.

Hong Kong is a place that provokes questions, some without answers. Those five-star hotels and soaring skyscrapers are first world, but those crumbling tenements look third world, don't they? Where has all the oil-slick slow traffic come from and where on earth is it going? How do seven million people fit on this tiny speck of land? And how do they decide where to eat in The City of 10,000 Restaurants? How can a simmering tureen of tripe stock look so evil yet smell so good? And what, exactly, is in the food product you saw in the supermarket labelled 'vegetarian gizzard'?

Pondering, you reach the water and stare across to Hong Kong Island. Nothing has quite prepared you for the spectacle up close: freighters and motor junks forever plying their harbour trade and, beyond them, a *Futurama* cityscape rising from near vertical jungle slopes.

After this sensory wave has rolled over you, there's no option but to start swimming with the tide in this energetic city of merchants, chancers and grifters. You soon learn that Hong Kong rewards those who grab experience by the scruff of the neck, who try that bowl of shredded jellyfish, who consume conspicuously, who roar with the Happy Valley punters as the winner thunders home. It rewards, too, those with the yen to explore centuries-old temples in half-deserted walled villages or to stroll surf-beaten beaches far from all the neon and steel and people.

It's an intoxicating place – spectacular, exotic and accessible. If you're visiting for business, you'll find pleasure sneaks up on you. If you're visiting for pleasure, there's no shortage of locals who make it their business to please.

Top Stroll through the serene Hong Kong Zoological & Botanical Gardens (p44) **Bottom** Jump aboard a traditional Chinese-style boat to get an excellent vantage point from which to take in the spectacle of the city

>HIGHLIGHTS

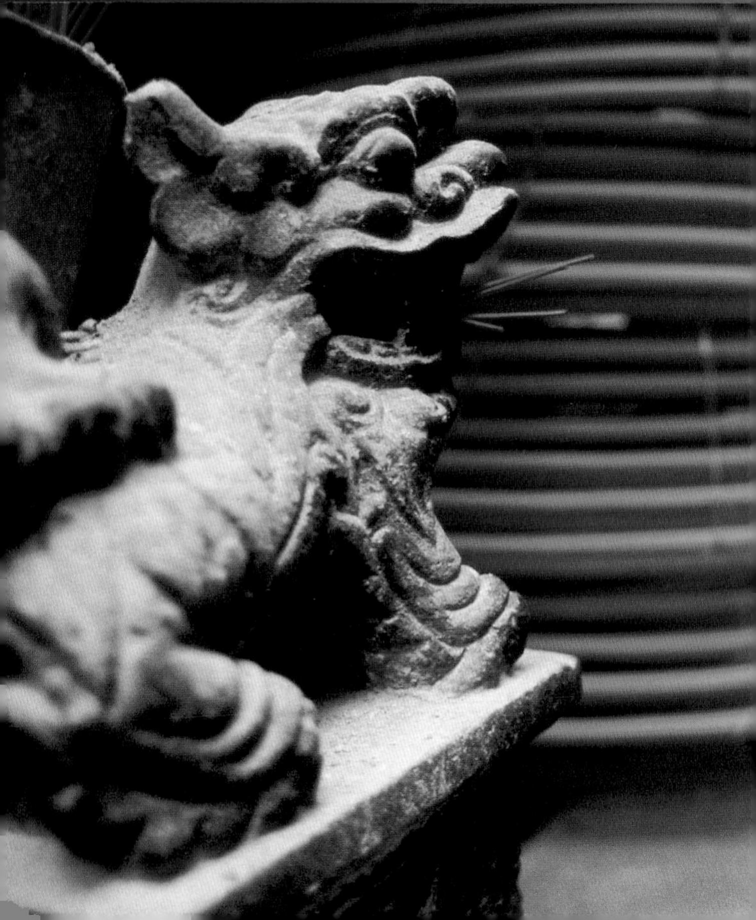

Burning incense to bring good fortune in the streets above Soho

HIGHLIGHTS

>1 STAR FERRY
JUMP ABOARD FLOATING HISTORY IN VICTORIA HARBOUR

You can't say you've 'done' Hong Kong until you've taken a ride on the implausibly inexpensive Star Ferry (p189). For a mere $2 you can board the upper deck of one of this small fleet of diesel-electric boats first launched in 1888. With names like *Morning Star, Celestial Star* and *Twinkling Star,* the ferries are most romantic at night. The boats are festively strung with lights, the city buildings beam onto the rippling water, the frenzy of Hong Kong by day has eased (somewhat) and Hong Kong Island bathes the harbour in its neon glow. If possible, try to take the trip on a clear night from Kowloon side to Central; it's not half as dramatic in the other direction. The trip takes about nine minutes (as long as it used to take to read the now defunct *Hong Kong Star,* a lowbrow tabloid newspaper, it was said), and departures are very frequent. Indeed, morning and evening, the Star Ferry is a genuinely useful and commonly used way for local people to hop from island to mainland and back again.

>2 HONG KONG VIEWS
OPEN YOUR EYES TO AMAZING VISTAS

It's hard not to revert to cliché, purple prose and overblown superlatives when attempting to describe the Hong Kong skyline and harbour. But words, and also photographs, really do fail to convey the rush of energy you get from taking in this futuristic megacity's outline and the amazing natural topography on which it's built. You need distance and perspective to do this properly and getting as high as you can (we mean physically) is one good way to enjoy this simple thrill. Head for the Bank of China Tower (p42) designed by China-born American architect IM Pei in 1990. Take the express lift to the 43rd floor from where you'll be rewarded with a panoramic view over Hong Kong. From here you are about the same height as the Hongkong & Shanghai Bank (p44) to the northwest. It's a pity that you aren't allowed to go any higher, as it's exciting swaying with the wind at the top. Even higher (though arguably not as dramatic) is the view from the windows of the Hong Kong Monetary Authority Information Centre on the 55th floor of the Two International Finance Centre (p46). For perhaps the ultimate show-stopping view, stand at the harbour edge in Tsim Sha Tsui (p112) and take in Hong Kong Island's skyscrapers' gradient-defying march up steep jungle slopes by day, and by night marvel at its captivating neon lightshow.

>3 WET MARKET
REACH SENSORY OVERLOAD IN THE WET MARKET'S COLOUR, AROMA AND GORE

Prepare to have your senses (and maybe sensibilities) assailed if you tour a wet market, places that feed Hong Kong's appetite for fresh (and, in many cases, live) food. Stalls of exotic fresh produce – star fruit, custard apples and dragon fruit – are piled high next to ones selling other local delicacies and staples, such as preserved eggs (the ready-to-eat greenish-black ones packed in a mixture of ash, lime and salt and buried for 100 days) or fresh white bean curd scooped still steaming from wooden pails. Be warned, though: those of a squeam-ish disposition might find wet markets unnerving. All manner of live crustaceans and reptiles lie blinking and squirming in baskets while live fish are sliced lengthways, their exposed hearts left beating on the slab. Our favourite is the outdoor Graham St Market (p56). Walk up from Queen's Rd Central (or down from Hollywood Rd) and prepare yourself for the cacophony and bustle, and the press of people linger-ing over, discussing and bargaining for food.

>4 TRAMS
ROCK & ROLL ALONG HONG KONG ISLAND'S NORTHERN COAST

It doesn't matter how many times we visit Hong Kong Island, a ride on a tram (p188) still offers a thrill right up there with the Star Ferry. Yes it's slow, not air-conditioned and it's fully exposed to the noise and bustle, but that's part of the appeal. For a couple of dollars, you'll make stately progress through a sliver of Hong Kong Island, your journey along the tram tracks offering a mesmeric and slowly scrolling urban panorama. These 164 tall, narrow streetcars comprise the world's only fully double-decker tramcar fleet, and they roll (and rock) along 13km of track from Kennedy Town in the west to Shau Kei Wan in the east, carrying almost a quarter of a million passengers a day. Try to get a seat at the front window on the upper deck for a first-class view while rattling through the crowded streets. Tall passengers will find it uncomfortable standing up as the ceiling is low, but there is more space at the rear of the tram on both decks. And be prepared to elbow your way through the crowd to alight, particularly on the lower deck.

>5 SHEUNG WAN
SHUFFLE THROUGH SHEUNG WAN'S OLD-SHANGHAI–STYLE HISTORIC ALLEYS

A short distance from Central's sharp, shiny edges but seemingly a world away, the streets of Sheung Wan (p40) form Hong Kong Island's old Chinese heart. It's a vibrant, colourful area that's best explored on foot. Although high-rise development is creeping west from Central, there's still a much more Chinese and old-fashioned character to the area and nary a shopping mall in sight. Follow your nose along Queens Rd West to the area around Wing Lok St and you've found the source of the area's pervasive fishy smell: the profusion of dried seafood and Chinese medicine wholesalers. Towering above the bins of dried bivalves and small fry, the piles of dried shark fins are a stark sign of their popularity in Hong Kong as a high-status delicacy, particularly at wedding receptions and other banquets. Several shops in the area also seem to base their business entirely on the sale of ginseng roots or swallow's nests, gathered at great risk high up in Malay sea caves. The latter are constructed entirely of swallow's

spittle, and are used in a number of Chinese dishes but most commonly for bird's nest soup, also commonly served as an entrée at formal dinners. Slightly uphill from here, the further western reaches of Hollywood Rd are also worth exploring for more interesting nooks and shops, including ones selling paper votives (such as Hell banknotes) burned to keep the dead in pocket money. The incense-filled Man Mo Temple (p45) is a nearby sight and opposite this you'll find Upper Lascar Row, also known as Cat St (p42), another traditional hunting ground for antiques, bric-a-brac and junk.

HK SEAFOOD: THE CATCH

When you see the piles of shark fins on sale in Sheung Wan, you won't be surprised to learn that half the world's shark species are now endangered. While scientists and conservation groups push for global limits on numbers caught, diners wishing to eat sustainably should avoid the soup the fins are commonly used to make. Regrettably many other fish served up in Hong Kong are also on the endangered list. To find out which are threatened and how to best avoid these, consult the website of the **Worldwide Fund for Nature** (wwf.org.hk) for a guide to eating sustainable seafood.

>6 HAPPY VALLEY RACES
A NIGHT AT THE RACES IN HAPPY VALLEY

They advise you not to get your hair cut on a Wednesday in Hong Kong, as the scissor-wielding barber will be more intent on the horse racing on TV than your scalp. It's easy to believe if you visit Happy Valley on race night. Beneath the twinkling lights of the surrounding high-rises, you'll see Hong Kong's citizens momentarily abandon their exterior poise as they yell their horse home (or curse the donkey they backed). Thousands attend and horse racing is still the main game in town, worth more than US$1 billion annually. The first horse races were held at the Happy Valley Racecourse (see boxed text, p89) in 1846. Now there are about 80 meetings a year split between the racecourse here and the newer and larger (but less atmospheric) one at Sha Tin in the New Territories. The racing season runs from September to early July. If you've been in Hong Kong for less than 21 days and are over 18 years of age, you can buy a tourist ticket, which allows you to jump the queue, sit in the members' enclosure and walk around next to the finish area. Make sure to bring along your passport as proof. Another option is to join the Come Horseracing tour (p192).

>7 PENINSULA HOTEL

TAKE A SIP OF LUXURY AT HONG KONG'S LEGENDARY HOTEL

For service as smooth as it comes, a regal atmosphere and a string quartet discreetly sawing away upstairs, afternoon tea at the Peninsula offers an affordable taste of the luxury Hong Kong. Undeniably one of the world's great hotels, the Peninsula (p110) is both a landmark and a Hong Kong icon. Though it was being called 'the finest hotel east of Suez' a few years after opening in 1928, the Peninsula was in fact one of several prestigious hostelries across Asia where everybody who was anybody stayed, up there with the likes of Raffles in Singapore, the Peace (then the Cathay) in Shanghai and the Strand in Rangoon (now Yangon). If you plan to take tea, dress neatly (no jacket required, though) and be prepared to queue for a table. While you're waiting, salivate at the sight of everyone else's cucumber sandwiches, scones and dainty cakes. The price of afternoon tea, served from 2pm to 7pm daily, for one is $255 and it's $360 per couple. It attracts a mixed clientele – from Japanese tourists to *tai tais* (any married women but especially the leisured wives of wealthy businessmen), who grab the most prominent tables, sip and gossip with their friends (mostly via mobile phones). When you're through (and to bring yourself back to earth) cross Nathan Rd and have a look round the shopping arcade of the rabbit warren called Chungking Mansions (p108).

>8 THE PEAK

A BREATH OF FRESH AIR AT THE TOP OF HONG KONG ISLAND

The Peak (p74), Hong Kong Island's highest point, has been *the* place to live ever since the British came here in the 19th century. The taipans built summer houses here to escape the heat and humidity (it's usually about 5°C cooler than down below). The Peak remains the most fashionable – and expensive – area to live in Hong Kong and is the territory's foremost tourist destination. Not only is the view from the summit one of the most spectacular cityscapes in the world, it's a good way to get Hong Kong into perspective. And the only way up, as far as we are concerned, is via the Peak Tram (see pp188-9 and boxed text, p77).

Rising above the Peak Tram terminus is the seven-storey Peak Tower, an anvil-shaped building containing shops, restaurants, tourist tat and a viewing terrace. Opposite is the Peak Galleria, a three-storey mall of shops and restaurants. Like the tower, it's designed to withstand winds of up to 270km/h, theoretically more than the maximum velocity of a No 10 typhoon.

When people in Hong Kong refer to the Peak, they usually mean the plateau and surrounding residential area at about 400m. The summit, Victoria Peak (552m), is about 500m northwest of the Peak

Tram terminus up steep Mt Austin Rd. The governor's mountain lodge near the summit was burned to the ground by the Japanese during WWII, but the gardens remain and are open to the public.

You can walk around Victoria Peak without exhausting yourself. Harlech Rd and Lugard Rd slope together form a 3.5km loop that takes about an hour. If you feel like a longer stroll (and want to avoid the Peak Tram and its crowds on the way down), you can continue for a further 2km along Peak Rd to Pok Fu Lam Reservoir Rd, which leaves Peak Rd near the car park exit. This goes past the reservoir to the main Pok Fu Lam Rd, where you can get bus 7 back to Central. Another good walk leads down to Hong Kong University. First walk to the west side of Victoria Peak by taking either Lugard or Harlech Rds. After reaching Hatton Rd, follow it down. The descent is steep, but the path is clear.

PRICES AT A PEAK

If you're in the market for one of the world's priciest homes, head to the Peak's Severn Rd, the second-most expensive street on earth (only beaten to top spot by Monaco's Ave Princess Grace). The best properties, those commanding the heights and so the most spectacular city views, cost around $120,000 per sq metre. Can we interest you in the four-bedroom place (plus maid's room) at No 23, which was valued a while back at $500m? Or perhaps you'd prefer to rent it, a snip at $380,000 per month (maid not included).

>9 SIK SIK YUEN WONG TAI SIN TEMPLE
PRAY FOR GOOD FORTUNE IN NEW KOWLOON

Sik Sik Yuen Wong Tai Sin Temple (p133) is an explosion of colour with red pillars, bright-yellow roofs and green-and-blue latticework. What's particularly striking is its popularity with locals. If you visit in the late afternoon or early evening, you can watch the hordes praying and divining the future with *chim,* bamboo 'prediction sticks' that must be shaken out of a box on to the ground and then read (they're available free to the left of the main temple). Behind the main temple and to the right are the Good Wish Gardens, replete with colourful pavilions (the hexagonal Unicorn Hall with carved doors and windows is the most beautiful), zigzag bridges and artificial ponds. Just below the main temple and to the left as you enter the complex is an arcade filled with dozens of booths operated by fortune-tellers. Some speak decent English (and advertise the fact on signs above their counters), so if you really want to know what fate has in store for you, this is your chance. The busiest times at the temple are around the Chinese New Year, Wong Tai Sin's birthday (23rd day of the eighth month – usually in September) and on weekends, especially Friday evening.

>10 HONG KONG MUSEUM OF HISTORY

TAKE A TRIP BACK THROUGH TIME

Hong Kong, in case you hadn't noticed, is a city whose commercially minded movers and shakers have their eyes firmly on the future, never much minding if the past gets torn up. This makes the few remnants of the past – be they listed buildings and monuments or old-fashioned observances (such as a computer-shop owner tending a shrine to the Earth God Tou Tei in his shop) – precious indeed. 'The Hong Kong Story' at the Hong Kong Museum of History (p108) takes visitors on a fascinating walk through the territory's past via eight galleries, starting with the natural environment and prehistoric Hong Kong on the ground floor – about 6000 years ago, give or take a lunar year – and ending with the territory's return to China in 1997 and a moving video collage of Hong Kong through the ages on the 2nd. Along the way you'll encounter replicas of village dwellings; traditional Chinese costumes and beds; a re-creation of an entire arcaded street in Central from 1881, including an old Chinese medicine shop; a tram from 1913; and film footage of WWII, including recent interviews with Chinese and foreigners taken prisoner by the Japanese. A favourite exhibit remains the jumble of toys and collectables from the 1960s and '70s when 'Made in Hong Kong' meant 'Christmas stocking trash'.

>11 DIM SUM

INDULGE IN SOME YUM-YUM YUM CHA

Yum cha (literally 'drink tea') is the usual way to refer to dim sum, the uniquely Cantonese 'meal' eaten as breakfast, brunch or lunch between about 7am and 3pm. Eating dim sum is a social occasion, consisting of many separate dishes that are meant to be shared. The bigger your group, the better. Dim sum delicacies are normally steamed in small bamboo baskets. The baskets are stacked up on trolleys and rolled around the dining room. You don't need a menu (though these exist, too, but are almost always in Chinese); just stop the waiter and choose something from the trolley. It will be marked down on a bill left on the table. Don't try to order everything at once. Each trolley has a different selection, so take your time and order as they come. It's said that there are about a thousand dim sum dishes, but you'd be doing well to sample 10 in one sitting.

char siu bau – steamed barbecued pork buns
cheung fun – steamed rice-flour rolls with shrimp, beef or pork
ching chau si choi – fried green vegetable of the day
chun gun – fried spring rolls
fan guo – steamed dumplings with shrimp and bamboo shoots
fu pei gun – crispy bean-curd rolls
fun guo – steamed dumplings with pork, peanuts and coriander
fung jau – fried chicken's feet

TEA TOO

Choosing the tea is as important to Chinese people as selecting the dishes at yum cha. Basically there are three main types: green (or unfermented) tea (luk cha); black tea (hung cha in Chinese, which translates as 'red tea'), which is fermented and includes the ever-popular bole; and oolong (wu lung cha) tea, which is semifermented. In between are countless scented variations, such as heung ping (jasmine), which is a blend of black tea and flower petals. When your teapot is empty and you want a refill, signal the waiter by taking the lid off the pot and resting it on the handle.

har gau – steamed shrimp dumplings
loh mei fan – sticky rice wrapped in lotus leaf
pai guat – small braised spareribs with black beans
san juk ngau yok – steamed minced beef balls
siu mai – steamed pork and shrimp dumplings

Dim sum restaurants are normally brightly lit and very large and noisy – it's rather like eating in an aircraft hangar. See boxed text, p163, for a list of the best.

>12 HONG KONG PARK
ESCAPE TO THE CITY'S RAINFOREST AVIARY

Deliberately designed to look anything but natural, Hong Kong Park (p80) is one of the most unusual parks in the world, emphasising artificial creations, such as its fountain plaza, conservatory, artificial waterfall, indoor games hall, playground, t'ai chi garden, viewing tower, museums and an arts centre. For all its artifice, the eight-hectare park is beautiful in its own weird way and, with a wall of skyscrapers on one side and mountains on the other, makes for dramatic photographs. Its best feature by far is the Edward Youde Aviary, named after a much-loved former governor (1982–87) and China scholar who died suddenly while in office. Home to hundreds of birds representing some 150 different species, the aviary is a huge and convincing re-creation of tropical forest habitat. Visitors walk along a wooden bridge suspended 10m above ground, at eye level with tree branches where most of the birds are; there are about a dozen viewing platforms. Schedule your visit in the morning, when the birds are most active. Volunteers from the Hong Kong Bird Watching Society lead visitors through the park and aviary, identifying various exotic species, including sulphur-coloured cockatoos, Chinese bulbuls and blue magpies.

>13 TEMPLE STREET NIGHT MARKET
DINNER AND A SHOW FOR A SONG

Temple St, named after the temple dedicated to Tin Hau at its centre, hosts the liveliest night market (p124) in Hong Kong. It used to be known as 'Men's St' because the market only sold men's clothing and to distinguish it from the 'Ladies' Market' on Tung Choi St (p125) to the northeast. Though there are still a lot of items on sale for men, vendors don't discriminate – anyone's money will do. But don't just come here to shop; this is also a place for eating and entertainment. For street food, head for Woo Sung St, running parallel to the east, or to the section of Temple St north of the temple towards Man Ming Lane. You can get anything from a fried snack to go or a simple bowl of noodles to a full meal served at your very own kerbside table. There are a few seafood and hotpot restaurants as well, or you might pop into Mido (p127), Hong Kong's best known *cha chan tang* (café with local dishes). You'll also find a surfeit of fortune-tellers and herbalists and some free, open-air Cantonese opera performances here. The market officially opens in the afternoon and closes at midnight, but it is at its best from about 7pm to 10pm, when it's clogged with stalls and people. If you want to carry on, visit the colourful wholesale fruit market (corner Shek Lung and Reclamation Sts), which is always a hive of activity from midnight to dawn.

>14 HONG KONG WETLAND PARK

HIDES AND FEATHERS IN THE MARSHES

If you're a real bird fancier, the Mai Po Marsh, a fragile, 270-hectare ecosystem in the northwestern New Territories and one of the largest natural habitats for wildlife in Hong Kong, is the best place to meet up with thousands of your feathered friends. But it's reserved for serious aficionados and is not the easiest place to reach. The more accessible Hong Kong Wetland Park (p138) contains a huge visitor centre called Wetland Interactive World, with three major galleries and a surfeit of hands-on and educational exhibits, a theatre and a resource centre. Outside there are four brief boardwalk walking trails through marshland and mangrove swamps, complete with viewing platforms and bird hides, and a discovery centre – all in all, a kind of high-tech Mai Po Marsh. The park is also now the home of Pui Pui, the irascible pet crocodile that escaped and managed to find his way to the Shan Pui River in Yuen Long, eluding would-be captors from Hong Kong, China and Australia for seven not-so-snappy months in 2004. Pui Pui seems content in his 'furnished' tank at the start of the nature trails but, like us, is no doubt unimpressed with the backdrop of Shenzhen on the mainland belching out pollution.

>HONG KONG DIARY

No matter what the time of year, you're almost certain to find some colourful festival or event occurring in Hong Kong. The choices seem endless — from long-established cultural events, like the Hong Kong Arts Festival, to traditional celebrations, such as the Dragon Boat Festival. Major sporting events such as the Hong Kong Rugby World Cup Sevens bring excitement and hordes of revellers, but nothing is quite as colourful as Hong Kong's traditional Chinese holidays, especially the Mid-Autumn Festival.

Giant lanterns light up the night for the Mid-Autumn Festival (p30)

JANUARY

Chinese New Year
www.discoverhongkong.com
Southern China's most important public
holiday (14 February 2010, 3 February 2011)
is welcomed in by flower markets, fireworks
and a huge international parade.

Hong Kong City Festival
www.hkfringe.com.hk
Get a taste of the city's culture during these
three weeks of eclectic performances both
local and from overseas.

FEBRUARY

Hong Kong Arts Festival
www.hk.artsfestival.org
A month-long extravaganza of music,
performing arts and exhibitions by hundreds
of local and international artists.

Spring Lantern Festival
www.discoverhongkong.com
This colourful lantern festival on the 15th
day of the first moon (mid- to late February,
28 February 2010) marks the end of the
lunar new year period and is a day for lovers.

Local children play an important part in the parade for the Cheung Chau Bun Festival

MOVEABLE FEASTS

Many Chinese red-letter days, both public holidays and privately observed affairs, go back hundreds, even thousands, of years, and the true origins of some are often lost in the mists of time. Dates vary from year to year, so if you want to time your visit to coincide with a particular event, check the website of the **Hong Kong Tourism Board** (www.discoverhongkong .com). In modern day Hong Kong there's a festival for everything: film and the arts, salsa, winter, all things French, Italian, Spanish and Mexican — even shopping gets its own spot on the calendar.

MARCH

Hong Kong Art Walk

www.hongkongartwalk.com
More than 40 galleries throw open their doors.

Hong Kong Rugby World Cup Sevens

www.hksevens.com.hk
This seven-a-side tournament attracts teams and spectators from all over the world.

Man Hong Kong International Literary Festival

www.festival.org.hk
Features novelists, short-story writers and poets from around the region and world.

Hong Kong International Film Festival

www.hkiff.org.hk
Screenings of almost 250 films from 40 countries worldwide.

APRIL

Ching Ming

www.discoverhongkong.com
A family celebration (4 April 2009, 5 April 2010) when people visit and clean the graves of ancestors.

Birthday of Tin Hau

www.discoverhongkong.com
This festival honours the patroness of sailors and fisherfolk — one of the territory's most popular goddesses.

MAY

Birthday of Lord Buddha

www.discoverhongkong.com
On this public holiday (2 May 2009, 21 May 2010) Buddha's statue is taken from the various monasteries and temples around Hong Kong and ceremonially bathed in scented water.

Cheung Chau Bun Festival

www.cheungchau.org
This is an unusual festival (2 May 2009, 29 May 2010) involving buns that is observed uniquely on the island of Cheung Chau (p142).

JUNE

Dragon Boat Festival

www.discoverhongkong.com

This festival (28 May 2009) commemorates the death of a 3rd-century-BC poet-statesman who hurled himself into a river to protest against a corrupt government. Dragon boat races are held throughout the territory but the most famous are at Stanley.

JULY

Hong Kong Fashion Week for Spring/Summer

http://hkfashionweekss.tdctrade.com

This is the spring-summer section of the biannual Hong Kong Fashion Week. Autumn-winter fashion week is held in January.

AUGUST

Hungry Ghost Festival

www.discoverhongkong.com

Marks the day when the gates of hell are opened and restless spirits are freed for two weeks to walk the earth. Paper 'hell' money and votives in the shape of cars, houses and clothing are burned on the last day.

SEPTEMBER

Mid-Autumn Festival

www.discoverhongkong.com

Held on the 15th night of the eighth moon (3 October 2009, 22 September 2010), this colourful festival involves eating little round 'moon' cakes while gazing at the full moon.

OCTOBER

Cheung Yeung

www.discoverhongkong.com

This festival (26 October 2009, 16 October 2010) is based on a Han dynasty story, where an oracle advised a man to take his family to a high place to escape a plague. Many people still head for the hills on this day and also visit the graves of ancestors.

NOVEMBER

Hong Kong International Cricket Sixes

www.hksixes.com

This two-day tournament pits Hong Kong's top cricketers against select teams from the eight Test-playing nations.

LO TAI FOOK EXPERT FORTUNE T

WELL KNOWN UNDER HEAVEN

FORTUNE-TELLING FROM PALM

FORTUNE TELLING BY FEELING

TO SUBSCRIBE ALL ONE'S LIFE

TELLING T___ ___ND FUTURE

MAKE NO ___ OF CITERIO

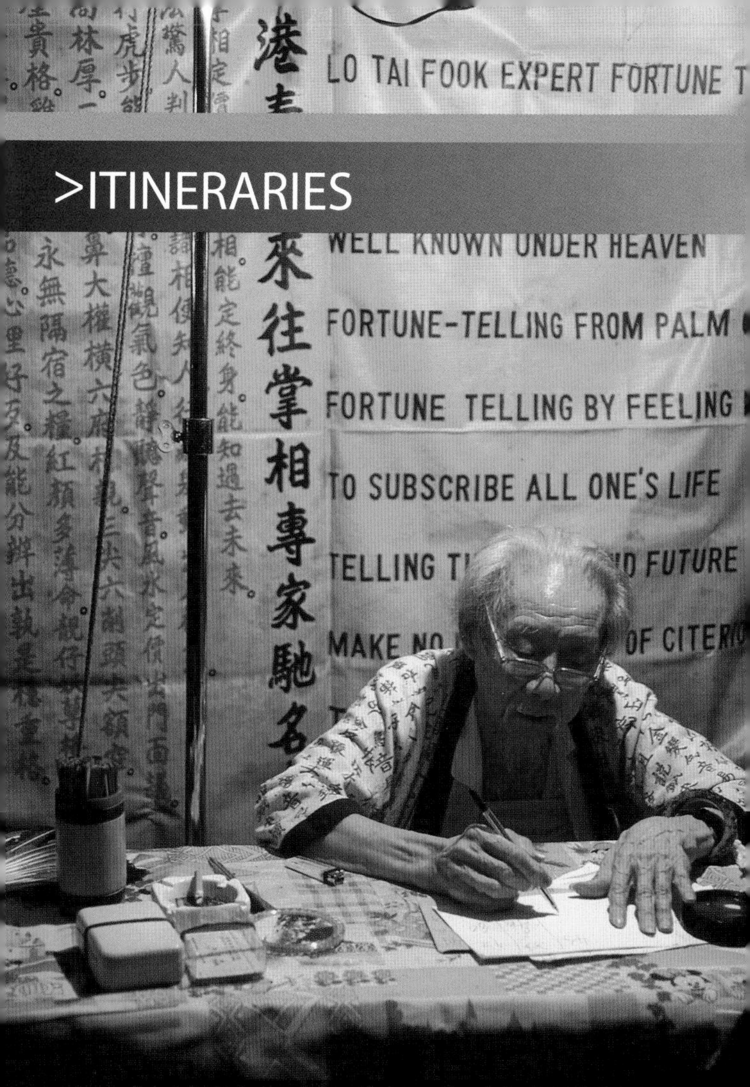

Find out what fate has in store – meet with a fortune teller at the Temple St Night Market (p124)

ITINERARIES

Whether you have a few hours to kill between flights or several days to enjoy, Hong Kong's super-efficient transport system and the city's compact nature means you can be sure to spend your leisure time profitably in the city and the wild areas on its fringes.

ONE DAY

Catch the Peak Tram up to the Peak (p74) for fine views of the city and a morning constitutional along the summit's circular path. Back down the hill take a stroll through Hong Kong Park (p80) before taking a tea break at the Lock Cha Tea Shop (p49) in the KS Lo Gallery. A lift in the Island Shangri-La Hong Kong Hotel will take you down to Pacific Place (p78) for some shopping. Take the westernmost exit from Pacific Place to emerge close to Wing Fung St for lunch at Xi Yan Sweets (p84) or a light lunch at Naturo+ (p84). Before you've finished nosing around this corner of Wan Chai relax over a drink at The Pawn (p88) before taking the Mass Transit Railway (MTR) to Central and weighing up the many options for dinner in Lan Kwai Fong and Soho (p61).

TWO DAYS

If your stay in Hong Kong amounts to a weekend, on day two take the Star Ferry (p189) to Tsim Sha Tsui to the Hong Kong Museum of History (p108). Meander over Nathan Rd for a stroll in Kowloon Park, then head south for lunch and views at Hutong (p117). Nip across to Harbour City for shopping at Lane Crawford (p113) or into Star House for Chinese crafts (p113) and computer bargains (p115) until you're ready for afternoon tea at the Peninsula Hotel (p110). Wander up to Yau Ma Tei (p122) and the Jade Market (p124). A mere hop, skip and slip northeast is Temple St Night Market (p124), where you can sample street food, have your fortune told and, if you're lucky, catch some open-air Cantonese opera.

THREE DAYS

On the third day, wander around Central and Sheung Wan (p40), poking your head into traditional shops (p14). The Macau Ferry Terminal is just

Top The Peak tram (p18) traverses the steep incline from Central to the Peak **Bottom** Savour the flavour – and the health benefits – of some freshly brewed tea at Lock Cha Tea Shop (p49)

across the road – why not hop aboard? Have lunch at the Clube Militar de Macau (p151) before visiting the embarrassment of sights and attractions around the Largo do Senado (p148) or trying your luck at the Wynn Macau Casino (p154). Walk along Rua Central through much of the Unesco-listed 'Historic Centre of Macau' (p148) and finish with a meal at Restaurante Litoral (p151). Back in Hong Kong spend the evening carousing in Lan Kwai Fong (p65).

ISLAND ESCAPADE
Hong Kong's crowds – everywhere at all times and always directly in your path – can become wearing. Escape them by fleeing to Lantau: take the MTR to Tung Chung and board the Ngong Ping Skyrail (p143) to Ngong Ping and the Tian Tan Buddha (p143). After a vegetarian lunch at the canteen of Po Lin Monastery (p144) board bus 21 for the traditional village of Tai O (p143). Bus 1 will return you to Mui Wo (Silvermine Bay) and the ferry to Central. Along the way, get off at Upper Cheung Sha beach (p143) for a swim or stroll.

RAINY DAY
If the rain has set in determinedly, trying to take in the sights is no fun as you weave and dodge through a thousand low-flying umbrella spikes. Take your pick from the museums of Tsim Sha Tsui (p108) to while away the best part of a day, string out a luxurious afternoon tea at the Peninsula Hotel (p110), take shelter deep in the gilded heart of Central's shopping malls (p47), many of them connected by walkways, or simply make a dash for one of the bars of Lan Kwai Fong and Soho (p65) in time for the lengthy happy hour.

FOR FREE
When the only thing in your pocket is 'shrapnel' (the little brown coins that make up $1), don't despair. Admission to places like the Flagstaff House Museum of Tea Ware (p80) in Hong Kong Park and the Hong Kong Heritage Discovery Centre in Kowloon Park (p110) is always gratis, but Wednesday is 'admission free' day at six museums: Hong Kong Heritage Museum (p138), Hong Kong Museum of Art (p108), Hong Kong Museum of Coastal Defence (see boxed text, p96), Hong Kong Museum of History (p108), Hong Kong Science Museum (p109) and Hong Kong Space Museum (p109), excluding the Space Theatre. For something

FORWARD PLANNING

Three weeks before you go Bag the best hotel rooms early. Hong Kong can fill up, especially during the conference and exhibition seasons in spring and autumn. See hotels .lonelyplanet.com for hotel bookings; get to know what's going on – both in the headlines and after hours – online by reading the local media, such as *South China Morning Post* at www.scmp.com.hk, *Hong Kong Standard* at www.thestandard.com.hk and *Time Out* at www.timeout.com.hk for its weekly listings; check to see if your visit coincides with any major holidays or festivals (p27); make sure your passport and other documents are in order.

One week before you go Book tickets for any major concerts or shows that might interest you at places like Hong Kong City Hall (p53), the Hong Kong Cultural Centre (p121) or the Fringe Club (p71); book that table at Petrus (p84) or M at the Fringe (p64).

The day before you go Reconfirm your flight; check the Hong Kong websites for any last-minute changes or cancellations at entertainment venues; buy some Hong Kong dollars; cancel the milk.

more spectacularly dramatic, head for the public viewing deck at the Bank of China (p42).

OPEN ALL HOURS

So, jetlag is playing havoc with your body clock. If it's very early in the morning, why not walk in a daze through Graham St Market (p56) and see the stallholders setting up before the 6am opening. At all hours the Hong Kong Island skyline from Tsim Sha Tsui (p112) is a marvel to sit and gape at, although if you're on the Hong Kong Island side after midnight, a taxi will be your only option to get here. Or perhaps you're desperate for a quick nap but don't want to pay for a hotel room. Never fear. Head to the Hong Kong Nap Centre (no, really) at the Delay No Mall (p94) and climb into one of its space-age sleep pods. After a late bite? How about Good Luck Thai Food (p63) on narrow Wing Wah Lane, open until 2am. If it's even later, try 369 Shanghai Restaurant (p83), which serves up good cheapo dumplings till 4am.

>NEIGHBOURHOODS

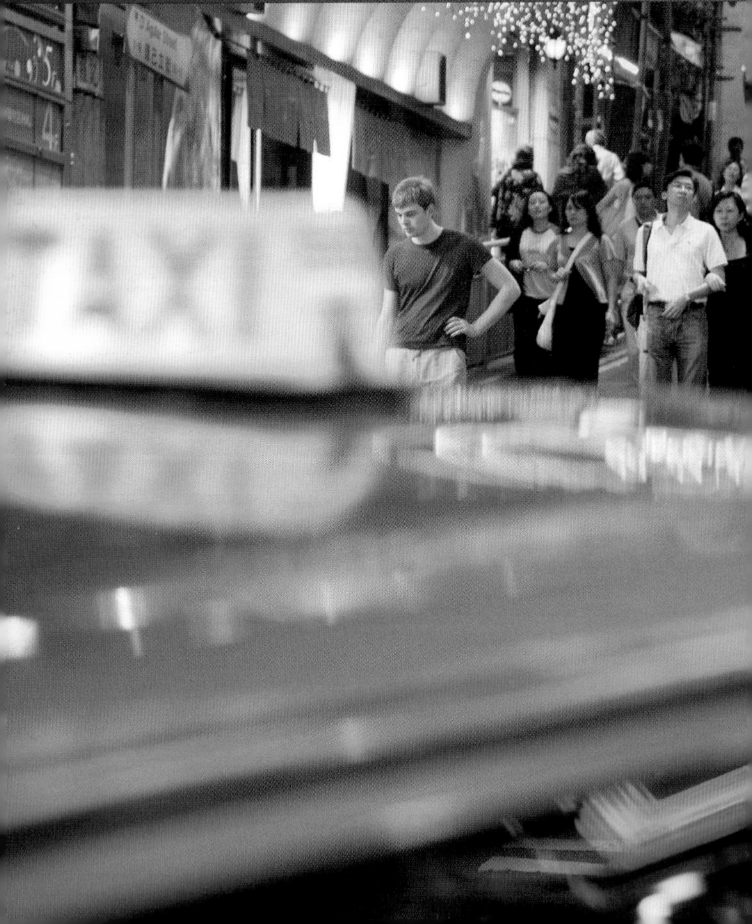

Lan Kwai Fong (p54) is a great place to experience the city's hustle and bustle

NEIGHBOURHOODS

Think of Hong Kong as being divided into four main areas: Hong Kong Island, Kowloon, the New Territories and the Outlying Islands. The beating commercial and social heart of Hong Kong lies in the first two of these areas – the Skyscraper-clad northern edge of Hong Kong Island and the busy district of Kowloon.

Central, on the northern side of Hong Kong Island, is where much of what happens (or is decided) in Hong Kong takes place; come here for business, sightseeing, and entertainment in Lan Kwai Fong and Soho.

Just to the west, Sheung Wan manages to retain the feel of pre-war Hong Kong in parts, and rising above Central are the Mid-Levels residential area and the Peak, home to the rich, the famous and the Peak Tram.

East of Central lies Admiralty, really just a cluster of office towers, hotels and shopping centres, and Wan Chai, a seedy red-light district during the Vietnam War but now a popular entertainment area. Beyond that lies Causeway Bay, the most popular shopping district on Hong Kong Island.

On the southern edge of the island are small popular seaside towns, including Stanley, with its fashionable restaurants, cafés and famous market.

North of Hong Kong Island is Kowloon, its epicentre the shopping, cultural and entertainment district of Tsim Sha Tsui. North of Tsim Sha Tsui are the working-class areas of Yau Ma Tei and Mong Kok, where you'll stumble across outdoor markets, Chinese pharmacies and mahjong parlours.

The New Territories, once Hong Kong's country playground, are today a mixed bag of housing estates and some surprisingly unspoiled rural areas and country parks containing temples, monasteries, old walled villages, wetlands, forested nature reserves and the idyllic Sai Kung Peninsula.

Among the so-called Outlying Islands accessible on a day trip from Hong Kong Island are: Cheung Chau, with its traditional village and fishing fleet; Lamma, celebrated for its restaurants and easy country walks; and Lantau, the largest island of all, with excellent beaches and country trails.

SOUTH CHINA SEA

Tung Ping Chau

Chek Chau Hau

Tai Pang Wan (Mirs Bay)

Tap Mun (Middle Channel)

Tap Mun Chau

Crooked Island

Double Island

Port Island

Tai Long Wan

Basalt Island

SHENZHEN

SHENCHEN SPECIAL ECONOMIC ZONE (SEZ)

Port Shelter

Lang Ha Wan

Clearwater Bay

Big Wave Bay

Tung Lung Chau

Po Toi

NEW TERRITORIES (p137)

NEW TERRITORIES

KWUN TONG

Junk Bay

KOWLOON

NEW KOWLOON (p131)

Tai Tam Bay

East Lamma Channel

Shau Wan

HONG KONG ISLAND

ISLAND SOUTH (p101)

SEE ENLARGEMENT

Tsing Yi

Ma Wan

Kau Yi Chau

West Lamma Channel

Lamma

East Brother

West Brother

Chek Lap Kok

LANTAU

NGONG PING

OUTLYING ISLANDS (p141)

Cheung Chau

Shek Kwu Chau

Soko Islands

Jau Lo Chau

Siu A Chau

Tai A Chau

Lantau Channel

0 6 km
0 3 miles

ENLARGEMENT

0 2 km

YAU MA TEI & MONG KOK (p123)

TSIM SHA TSUI & TSIM SHA TSUI EAST (p107)

CENTRAL & SHEUNG WAN, (p41)

LAN KWAI FONG & SOHO (p55)

THE MID-LEVELS & THE PEAK (p75)

Victoria Harbour

CAUSEWAY BAY (p91)

ADMIRALTY & WAN CHAI (p79)

MACAU

CHINA / Macau Peninsula

CHINA (Zhuhai SEZ)

MACAU (p147)

Taipa Island

Coloane Island

To Macau (20km)

0 2 km

>HONG KONG ISLAND: CENTRAL & SHEUNG WAN

The pulsing financial, political and retail heart of Hong Kong, sharp-suited Central is a heady mix of exclusive boutiques, peaceful parks, fine dining, modern corporate cathedrals and even a few historic colonial buildings (including a real cathedral marooned among the high-rises). Central is very much a 24-hour part of town. You can shop until late in a trio of huge, high-end, air-conditioned shopping malls and then stroll to nearby Lan Kwai Fong and Soho for a tempting variety and profusion of eating and drinking options. Arguably even more rewarding to explore, Sheung Wan still carries the echo of 'Old Shanghai' in places, with its traditional shops and old 'ladder streets' (steep inclined streets with steps). Stroll the length of Hollywood Rd from east to west and you'll experience a good cross section of both of these enticing neighbourhoods.

CENTRAL & SHEUNG WAN

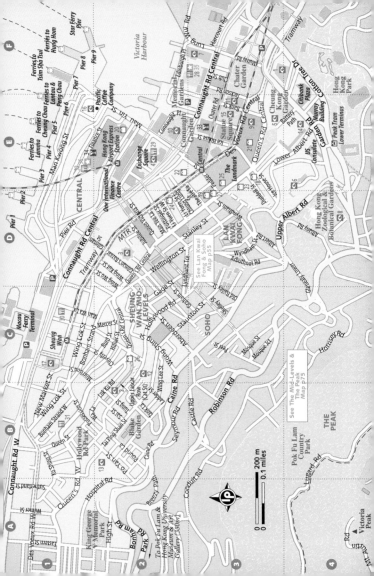

👁 SEE

🔵 BANK OF CHINA TOWER
中國銀行大廈
**1 Garden Rd, Central; admission free;
🕐 8am-6pm Mon-Fri; Ⓜ Central (exit J2)**
This stunning, 70-storey structure
is one Hong Kong's tallest and certainly most striking buildings. The
angular design gives the building
an aggressive stance that is said to
cast bad energies on nearby buildings. The views from the 43rd floor
are terrific (p11).

🔵 CAT ST MARKET 摩囉街
**Upper Lascar Row, Sheung Wan;
🕐 10am-6pm; 🚌 26 Ⓜ Sheung Wan**
Head to Upper Lascar Row (the
official name of what has become
known as Cat St and a pedestrian-
only laneway) for dozens of stalls
offering antiques, curios, cheap
jewellery, ornaments, carvings and
newly minted 'antique' coins. It's
a fun place to trawl through for a
trinket or two, but expect a lot of
rough, and few (if any), diamonds.

🔵 CENTER 中環中心
**99 Queen's Rd Central, Central; admission
free; Ⓜ Central (exit D) 🚊**
From close up, the protruding cor-
ners of this star-shaped, 73-storey
building built in 1998 appear to
cut into the structure. But what
really sets it apart is the hypnotic
nightly light show from almost
9000 neon tubes that send colour
lights cascading down the towering 'spines' every 15 minutes.

🔵 EXCHANGE SQUARE
交易廣場
**8 Connaught Place, Central; admission
free; Ⓜ Central (exit A) 🚌 🚊**
A good place to sit and relax beside
the fountain and several sculptures,
including one by Henry Moore. This
complex of three elevated office
towers above Central bus station
is home to the Hong Kong Stock
Exchange and many businesses.

🔵 FORMER FRENCH MISSION BUILDING
前法國外方傳道會大樓
**1 Battery Path, Central; admission free;
Ⓜ Central (exit K)**

BRUTAL BUILDING
Elegant it may be to some, but geomancers (practitioners of the art of feng shui)
see the Bank of China Tower as a huge
violation of its principles. The bank's
four triangular prisms are negative symbols in the geomancer's rule book; being
the opposite to circles, these contradict
what circles suggest – perfection and
(importantly in Hong Kong) prosperity.
Furthermore, the huge crosses on the
sides of the building suggest negativity
and its shape has been likened to a praying mantis (a threatening symbol), complete with radio masts as antennae.

Buddhas, beads and baubles – plenty to buy at the Cat St Market

Just behind pretty Cheung Kong Garden abutting St John's Cathedral is this charming structure built by an American trading firm in 1868. It served as the Russian consulate in Hong Kong until 1915 when the French Overseas Mission bought it and added a chapel and a dome. Today it houses the Court of Final Appeal, the highest judicial body in Hong Kong.

◉ GOVERNMENT HOUSE
香港禮賓府

☎ 2530 2003; Upper Albert Rd, Central; admission free; ☷ 1st Sun in Mar; 🚌 3B, 12, 23, 103

Parts of this one-time residence of Hong Kong's governors date back

to 1853, though the commanding tower was added by the Japanese during WWII. Both the current chief executive, Donald Tsang, and his predecessor, Tung Chee Hwa, refused to take up residence here, ostensibly because the feng shui isn't quite right.

◉ HONG KONG PLANNING & INFRASTRUCTURE GALLERY
香港規劃及基建展覽館

☎ 3102 1242; www.infrastructure gallery.gov.hk; 3 Edinburgh Pl, Central; admission free; ☷ 10am-6pm Wed-Mon; Ⓜ Central (exit K)

If you can't wait to see how the lengthy harbour remodelling project is going, this gallery, with

GREEN ENGINEERING

On Hong Kong Island only, and especially in Central and Sheung Wan, you'll see what are called 'wall trees', ancient banyan trees (mostly) sprouting from openings in stone retaining walls. To prevent landslides on steep Hong Kong Island, masonry workers from the late 19th century until well after WWII shored up many slopes adjacent to main roads with retaining walls. Open joints between the stones allowed strong species such as Chinese banyans to sprout, further strengthening the walls. Today slopes are, sadly but more reliably, stabilised by cement.

the mouthful of a name and next to the Low Block of Hong Kong City Hall (p53), takes visitors on a fascinating 18.5m 'walk' past recent, ongoing and future civil engineering, urban renewal and environment improvement projects in the territory.

◎ HONG KONG ZOOLOGICAL & BOTANICAL GARDENS 香港動植物公園

☎ 2530 0154; www.lcsd.gov.hk/parks/hkzbg; Albany Rd, Central; admission free; ☉ terrace gardens 6am-10pm, zoo & aviaries 6am-7pm, greenhouses 9am-4.30pm; 🚌 3B, 12, 40, 40M
These 5.6-hectare gardens, which first welcomed visitors in 1864, are a pleasant assembly of fountains, sculptures, green-

houses, a playground, a zoo and some fabulous aviaries. There are hundreds of species of birds in residence as well as exotic trees, plants and shrubs. The zoo is surprisingly comprehensive and one of the world's leading centres for the captive breeding of endangered species. Albany Rd divides the gardens, with the plants and aviaries to the east off Garden Rd and most of the animals to the west.

◎ HONGKONG & SHANGHAI BANK 香港上海匯豐銀行

HSBC; 1 Queen's Rd Central, Central; admission free; ☉ 9am-4.30pm Mon-Fri, 9am-12.30pm Sat; Ⓜ Central (exit K) 🚇
This 179m-tall glass-and-aluminium building is an innovative masterpiece. Locals call it the 'Robot Building' because you can see the chains and motors of the escalators and other moving parts whirring away inside. Structurally, the building is equally as radical, built on a 'coat-hanger' frame and boasts some wonderful feng shui according to master geomancers. See also p11 and the boxed text, opposite.

◎ JARDINE HOUSE 怡和大廈

1 Connaught Pl, Central; admission free; Ⓜ Central (exit A) 🚇
This 52-storey silver monolith was Hong Kong's first skyscraper

when it opened as the Connaught Centre in 1973. The building's 1750 porthole-like windows have earned it a less respectable Chinese nickname: 'House of 1000 Arseholes.'

◉ LEGISLATIVE COUNCIL BUILDING 立法會大樓
8 Jackson Rd, Central; admission free; Ⓜ Central (exit J1) 🖼
This colonnaded, domed neo-classical building is the former Supreme Court, built in 1912 of granite quarried on Stonecutter Island. Standing atop the pediment is a blindfolded statue of Themis, the Greek goddess of justice.

◉ MAN MO TEMPLE 文武廟
☎ 2540 0350; 124-126 Hollywood Rd, Sheung Wan; admission free; Ⓨ 8am-6pm; 🚌 26
Follow the smell of incense to this atmospheric, low-lit 'Civil and Martial' temple, one of the oldest in Hong Kong, and dedicated to a statesman of the 3rd century

BC called Man Cheung, who is worshipped as the god of literature, and a military deity called Kwan Yu, a soldier born in the 2nd century AD and now venerated as the red-cheeked god of war. See also p14.

◉ PARA/SITE ART SPACE 藝術空間
☎ 2517 4620; www.para-site.org.hk; 4 Po Yan St, Sheung Wan; admission free; Ⓨ noon-7pm Wed-Sun; Ⓜ Sheung Wan 🚌 26
This adventurous, artist-run space knows no boundaries when it comes to mixing media. Most art on display is local but there are occasional exhibitions by international artists as well.

◉ ST JOHN'S CATHEDRAL 約翰座堂
☎ 2523 4157; www.stjohnscathedral.org.hk; 4-8 Garden Rd, Central; admission free; Ⓨ 7am-6pm; Ⓜ Central (exit J2)
One of the few colonial structures still standing in Central and lost in

JUST LION THERE
Say hello to Stephen and Stitt, the pair of handsome bronze lions guarding the southern side of the Hongkong & Shanghai Bank (HSBC; opposite) headquarters. Named after the general managers of the two main branches in Hong Kong and Shanghai when they were cast in the 1930s, they have been through the wars (well one actually). Bullet scars from WWII still pepper their noble rumps and for years a piece of unexploded ordnance was lodged inside one of them until removed by a bomb disposal team. Rub their mighty paws for luck.

a forest of skyscrapers, this Anglican cathedral, built in the shape of a cross, is a relic of Hong Kong's colonial past. It suffered heavy damage during WWII; after the war the front doors were remade using timber salvaged from the British warship HMS *Tamar*, and the beautiful stained glass was replaced. A peaceful, cool and contemplative space. Enter from Battery Path.

☉ STATUE SQUARE
皇后像廣場
Chater Rd & Des Voeux Rd Central, Central; Ⓜ Central (exit K) 🚇
A chinless banker (and no that's not rhyming slang) is the only statue you'll find here. The rest of the carvings that once stood

in the square (British royals in the main) were carted off by the Japanese in WWII. In a city with Hong Kong's commercial drive and institutional indifference to culture, the slightly bathetic statue of Sir Thomas Jackson (a particularly successful Victorian-era manager of the Hongkong & Shanghai Bank) somehow fits right in. On the northern side of Chater Rd is the Cenotaph (1923) dedicated to Hong Kong residents killed during the two world wars.

☉ TWO INTERNATIONAL FINANCE CENTRE
國際金融中心二期
☎ 2878 1111; www.hkma.gov.hk; 8 Finance St, Central; admission free; ☽ 10am-6pm Mon-Fri, 10am-1pm Sat; Ⓜ Hong Kong (exit F) 🚇
At 88 storeys, Two IFC, soaring above the terminus of the Airport Express and Tung Chung MTR lines, is Hong Kong's tallest building and has been christened 'Sir Y K Pao's Erection', a reference to the owner of the development company that built the tower. You can get as far as the 55th floor by visiting the Hong Kong Monetary Authority Information Centre, which contains exhibition areas related to the Hong Kong currency, fiscal policy and banking history, and a research library. There are

WORTH THE TRIP
East of Sheung Wan in Pok Fu Lam district is the **Hong Kong University Museum & Art Gallery** (☎ 2241 5500; www.hku.hk/hkumag; Fung Ping Shan Bldg, 94 Bonham Rd; admission free; ☽ 9.30am-6pm Mon-Sat, 1.30-5.30pm Sun; 🚌 23, 40, 40M) containing important collections of ceramics and bronzes, plus a lesser number of paintings and carvings. There's an intriguing display of almost a thousand crosses made by Nestorians, a Christian sect that arose in Syria and moved into China during the 13th and 14th centuries.

You'll find no shortage of shopping options at the Two International Finance Centre Mall

guided tours at 2.30pm Monday to Friday and at 10.30am on Saturday. See also p11.

ⓒ WESTERN MARKET 西港城
323 Des Voeux Rd Central, Sheung Wan;
🕐 **9am-7pm;** Ⓜ **Sheung Wan (exit C)** 🚊

This three-storey Edwardian market (1906) reopened in 1991 as a shopping centre to house textile vendors driven out of the lanes linking Queen's Rd and Des Voeux Rd Central. The ground floor has modern shops selling curios, jewellery and toys; the 1st floor is given over mostly to bolts of cloth, including some decent silks. On the top floor there's a picturesque restaurant and ballroom dancing space.

🛍 SHOP

Sumptuous temples to couture and conspicuous consumption prosper inside Central's swish shopping malls (take your pick from the Princes Building, The Landmark or the IFC Malls), although you'll also find midrange clothing brands here. Hollywood Rd, which links Central and Sheung Wan, is particularly good for antiques, fine art and curios, while Stanley St in Central is the spot for quality film cameras. For an 'only-in-Hong-Kong' experience, visit Li Yuen St East and West, two narrow alleyways that link Des Voeux Rd Central with Queen's Rd Central, for a jumble of inexpensive clothing, handbags and jewellery.

🛒 BAPE STORE
Clothing & Accessories
☎ 2868 9448; 10 Queen's Rd Central, Central; Ⓜ Central 🕊
How Japanese cult label Bathing Ape's formerly hard-to-find T-shirts, trainers and other urban wear will sustain its cool reputation with huge flagship stores like this one is anyone's guess. Check out the underfloor footwear 'train' as you enter.

🛒 BLANC DE CHINE 源
Clothing & Accessories
☎ 2524 7875; Shop 201-203A, 2nd fl, Pedder Bldg, 12 Pedder St, Central; 🕒 10am-7pm Mon-Sat, noon-5pm Sun; Ⓜ Central 🕊

Silk dresses for her, men's traditional Chinese jackets, off the rack or made to measure, and an exquisite collection of satin bed linens are the specialities here.

🛒 DYMOCKS BOOKSELLERS
恬墨書舍 *Books*
☎ 2117 0360; www.dymocks.com.hk; Shop 2007-2011, 2nd fl, IFC Mall, 8 Finance St, Central; 🕒 9.30am-9.30pm; Ⓜ Central, Hong Kong 🕊
The large Australian chain offers a solid mainstream selection of page turners, travel books, magazines and, in particular, books of local interest. This is one of its seven Hong Kong branches.

🛒 HANART TZ GALLERY
漢雅軒 *Fine Art*
☎ 2526 9019; www.hanart.com; Room 202, 2nd fl, Henley Bldg, 5 Queen's Rd Central, Central; 🕒 10am-6.30pm Mon-Fri, 10am-6pm Sat; Ⓜ Central (exit K) 🕊
One of the most influential and innovative galleries in Hong Kong,

---

SUZIE WONG'S WARDROBE
Reach into any Hong Kong Chinese woman's closet and you're bound to find at least one cheongsam (*qipao* in Mandarin), the close-fitting sheath that is Hong Kong's national dress. It's worn on formal occasions, such as Chinese New Year gatherings, to work (restaurant receptionists and nightclub hostesses wear them), to school (cotton cheongsams are still the uniform at several colleges and secondary schools) or for the 'big day'. Modern Hong Kong brides may take their vows in white, but before they slip off for the honeymoon, they put on a red cheongsam.

TRADITIONAL MEDICINE

Chinese herbalists are popular in Hong Kong, selling general health tonics or, after a diagnosis, tailored brews for specific ailments. Why not try one? Ingredients might include deer's horn, tail and penis; snake skin; monkey's visceral organs; and ground dinosaur teeth. Drink up now.

Hanart shows contemporary Chinese art with a thoroughbred stable of figurative and conceptual painters, sculptors and video artists, many of them based in Hong Kong.

📖 HONG KONG BOOK CENTRE
Books
☎ 2522 7064; www.swindonbooks.com; Basement, On Lok Yuen Bldg, 25 Des Voeux Rd Central, Central; ⏲ 9am-6.30pm Mon-Fri, 9am-5.30pm Sat, 1-5pm Sun Jul & Aug; Ⓜ Central (exit B) 🚊
This basement shop has a vast selection of books and magazines, including a mammoth number of business titles.

👕 JOYCE
Clothing & Accessories
☎ 2810 1120; www.joyce.com; Ground fl, New World Tower, 16 Queen's Rd Central, Central; ⏲ 10.30am-7.30pm; Ⓜ Central 🚊
This multidesigner store is a good choice if you're short of time

rather than money: Issey Miyake, Alexander McQueen, Marc Jacobs, Comme des Garçons, Chloé, Pucci, Yohji Yamamoto and several Hong Kong fashion names are just some of the designers whose wearable wares are on display.

💍 KING FOOK JEWELLERY
景福珠寶 *Jewellery*
☎ 2822 8573; www.kingfook.com; Ground fl, King Fook Bldg, 30-32 Des Voeux Rd Central, Central; ⏲ 9.30am-7pm; Ⓜ Central 🚊
A shop and a spectacle in one, King Fook, with its grandiose gilded entrance, stocks a large range of watches, top-end fountain pens and gewgaws.

🎁 LIULIGONGFANG 琉璃工房
Gifts & Souvenirs
☎ 2973 0820; www.liuli.com; Shop 20-22, ground fl, Central Bldg, 1-3 Pedder St, Central; ⏲ 10am-7.30pm Mon-Sat, 10am-7pm Sun; Ⓜ Central 🚊
A store with exquisite coloured objects, both practical (vases, candle holders) and ornamental (Buddhism figurines, jewellery), from a renowned Taiwan glass sculptor.

☕ LOCK CHA TEA SHOP
樂茶軒 *Food & Drink*
☎ 2805 1360; Upper ground fl, 290b Queen's Rd Central (enter from Ladder St), Sheung Wan; ⏲ 11am-7pm; Ⓜ Sheung Wan (exit A2)

NEIGHBOURHOODS

HONG KONG ISLAND: CENTRAL & SHEUNG WAN

New and old combine to stylish effect at the exclusive Shanghai Tang

This favourite shop sells Chinese teas, tea sets, wooden tea boxes and well-presented gift packs of various cuppas. You can try before you buy.

LULU CHENG
Clothing & Accessories
☎ 2537 7515; Shop B63, Basement, Landmark Bldg, Central; Ⓜ Central
Local designer Lulu Cheng designs and makes sophisticated, understated women's casual wear and elegant evening gowns using natural fabrics, such as wool, cotton, silk and linen, in muted tones.

SHANGHAI TANG 上海灘
Clothing & Accessories
☎ 2525 7333; www.shanghaitang.com; Basement & ground fl, Pedder Bldg, 12 Pedder St, Central; ✆ 10am-8pm Mon-Sat, noon-6pm Sun; Ⓜ Central ⓡ
This stylish shop has sparked something of a fashion wave with its updated versions of traditional yet neon-coloured Chinese garments. It also sells accessories and delightful gift items.

🍴 EAT

🍴 CITY HALL MAXIM'S PALACE
大會堂美心皇宮
Dim Sum $$
☎ 2521 1303; 3rd fl, Low Block, Hong
Kong City Hall, 1 Edinburgh Pl, Central;
🕑 11am-3pm & 5.30-11.30pm Mon-Sat,
9am-11.30pm Sun; Ⓜ Central
You'll find the real Hong Kong
dim sum deal, with all its clatter
and clutter, in Hong Kong City
Hall on Saturday or Sunday
morning. Cacophonous but
delectable.

🍴 HUNAN GARDEN 洞庭樓
Hunanese $$$
☎ 2868 2880; 3rd fl, The Forum,
Exchange Sq, Connaught Rd Central,
Central; 🕑 11.30am-3pm & 5.30-
11.30pm; Ⓜ Central
This elegant place specialises in
spicy Hunanese cuisine, which
is often hotter than the Sichuanese variety. The Hunanese fried
chicken with chilli is excellent, as
are the seafood dishes.

🍴 KOREA HOUSE 梨花園
Korean $$
☎ 2544 0007; Ground fl, Honwell
Commercial Centre, 119-121 Connaught
Rd Central, Sheung Wan; 🕑 noon-11pm;
Ⓜ Sheung Wan
This comfortable restaurant serves
a delicious array of appetisers

(dried fish, pickles, kimchi) as side
dishes to the barbecue sizzling
at your table. Enter from Man Wa
Lane.

🍴 LEUNG HING RESTAURANT
兩興潮州海鮮飯店
Chiu Chow $$
☎ 2850 6666; 32 Bonham Strand
West, Sheung Wan; 🕑 11am-11pm;
Ⓜ Sheung Wan
The staple ingredients of Chiu
Chow cuisine (shellfish, goose and
duck) are extensively employed
and delectably prepared at this
very local place. Bring a native
speaker or use your hands.

🍴 LUNG KING HEEN 龍景軒
Chinese $$$
☎ 3196 8888; Four Seasons Hotel,
8 Finance St, Central; Ⓜ Central
It's not just the view alone that
you should come here for, it is
the plump and fresh crustaceans
and the divine roast duck ($560
each, good for six people to
share).

🍴 THREE SIXTY
Supermarket, Food Hall $
☎ 2111 4480; 3rd & 4th fl, The Landmark,
Central; Ⓜ Central 🍴
Organic and whole foods, tempt-
ing picnic goodies and a terrific
food court with cuisine from all
over the world on the upper floor.
An ideal spot for a swift lunch.

Giovanni Valenti
Concierge at the deluxe Mandarin Oriental hotel, Central

So what does a concierge do? We look after people from the moment they arrive at the airport. Whatever you need – a giant teddy bear, 99 yellow roses for your wife, or a table at the best restaurant – we'll organise it. The word 'no' does not exist, although we will decline illegal requests politely. **The sharp end of the hospitality business then?** Yes. A concierge is a combination of a host and a friend, sometimes a companion, maybe also a doctor or psychiatrist. It's all about understanding guests' moods and anticipating what they will need. Sometimes you're even like a priest; if people confide in you, you never betray that or name names. **Sounds like hard work?** Not to me. I love people. My guests are my life. I should have retired by now but this job is like my hobby. **So where do you go when you're not pampering the elite?** I go to the opera when there's any in town. The Cultural Centre (p121) and Hong Kong City Hall (opposite) are great venues.

🍸 DRINK

🍸 CAPTAIN'S BAR *Bar*
☎ 2522 0111; Ground fl, Mandarin Oriental, 5 Connaught Rd Central, Central; 🕒 11am-2am Mon-Sat, 11am-1am Sun; Ⓜ Central 🚻
This clubby, suited place remains just as comfortable and familiar as ever. It serves ice-cold draught beer in chilled silver mugs and some of the best martinis in town. A good place to linger and witness Hong Kong movers and shakers talking shop.

🍸 RED BAR *Bar*
☎ 8129 8882; L4, Two IFC, 8 Finance St, Central; 🕒 noon-midnight Mon-Thu, noon-3am Fri & Sat, noon-10pm Sun; Ⓜ Central
A fantastic combination of al fresco drinking and harbour views is hard to beat on Hong Kong Island. DJs playing funk and jazz turn up the volume as the weekend approaches.

⭐ PLAY

⭐ HONG KONG CITY HALL
香港大會堂
Live Music, Dance
☎ 2921 2840, bookings 2734 9009; www.cityhall.gov.hk; Low Block, 1 Edinburgh Pl, Central; tickets $80-750; Ⓜ Central 🚻
Built in 1962, Hong Kong City Hall is still a major cultural venue in Hong Kong, with concert and recital halls, a theatre and exhibition galleries.

⭐ SPA AT THE FOUR SEASONS *Health & Fitness*
☎ 3196 8888; www.fourseasons.com; Four Seasons Hotel, 8 Finance St, Central; Ⓜ Central
This vast (20,000 sq ft) and ultra high-end spa pretty much offers it all. As well as a comprehensive range of beauty, massage and health treatments, there's an ice fountain, hot cups, moxibustion and something called a herbal cocoon room.

NEIGHBOURHOODS

HONG KONG ISLAND: CENTRAL & SHEUNG WAN

>HONG KONG ISLAND: LAN KWAI FONG & SOHO

Lan Kwai Fong and Soho, actually parts of Central, form the dining and partying epicentre of Hong Kong Island. Much of Central's nightlife revolves around Lan Kwai Fong, a narrow alleyway doglegging south and then west from D'Aguilar St. In the not-so-distant past it was an area of squalid tenements, rubbish and rats, but it has since been scrubbed,

LAN KWAI FONG & SOHO

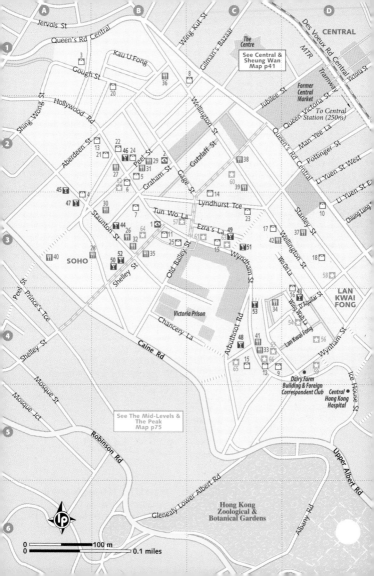

CENTRAL

The Centre
See Central &
Sheung Wan
Map p41

Jervois St

Queen's Rd Central

Wing Kut St

Gilman's Bazaar

Des Voeux Rd Central

MTR

Victoria St

Former
Central
Market

Kau U Fong

To Central
Station (250m)

Jubilee St

Queen Victoria St

Queen's Rd Central

Man Yee La

3
Gough St

36

20

Hollywood Rd

Shing Wong St

Wellington St

Pottinger St

Li Yuen St West

Li Yuen St E

Aberdeen St

22
13
21

46 24

Peel St

2

29

Graham St

5

Gutzlaff St

Cage St

38

60
39

Stanley St

Chiung Lung

27

6

45
47

4

30

7

14

Lyndhurst Tce

23

10

Staunton St

Tun Wo La

57

1

Ezra's La

49

17

37

Wellington St

Wo La

18

58

26
64
32

44

11

25

Old Bailey St

51

Wyndham St

42
51

LAN
KWAI
FONG

40

28

52
50

35

Shelley St

SOHO

Peel St

Prince's Tce

Victoria Prison

43

Wing Wah La

D'Aguilar St

34

53

54

Lan Kwai Fong

56

Shelley St

Chancery La

Arbuthnot Rd

48

41
33

66

15
65

12

9

Wyndham St

Ice House St

Mosque St

Caine Rd

Mosque Jct

See The Mid-Levels &
The Peak
Map p75

Robinson Rd

Dairy Farm
Building & Foreign
Correspondent Club

Central
Hong Kong
Hospital

Glenealy Lower Albert Rd

Hong Kong
Zoological &
Botanical Gardens

Upper Albert Rd

Albany Rd

0   100 m
0   0.1 miles

face-lifted and closed to traffic. Lan Kwai Fong's clientele tends to be relatively young and upwardly mobile, and expats mix easily with local business types and trendies. The action has spilled further up the hill all the way along Wyndham St, where you'll find a dozen or so smarter bars and restaurants, all of them abuzz almost every night of the week. Nearby Soho (short for 'south of Hollywood Rd') is more geared for dining than drinking. The area also offers shoppers a welcome and atmospheric contrast to the enclosed megamalls in nearby Central. Along Hollywood Rd you'll find fierce tomb guards and other ancient Chinese antiquities alongside classic and contemporary art. Soho meanwhile is becoming, almost by the day, a more interesting hunting ground for quirky independent clothes and interiors retailers.

👁 SEE

🔵 CENTRAL ESCALATOR
中環至半山自動扶梯
☎ 2523 7488; Cochrane St, cnr Shelley & Peel Sts, Central; admission free; 🕒 down 6-10am, up 10.20am-midnight; Ⓜ Central (exit C) 🚻

The world's longest covered outdoor people-mover is part commuter travelator, part sightseeing ride and part pick-up procession. It consists of elevated escalators, moving walkways and linking stairs on the 800m hill from Central's offices to the bedroom communities of the Mid-Levels. The best part is gliding by the Shelley St bars; there's just enough time to make flirtatious eye contact with the denizens within.

🔵 GRAHAM ST MARKET
Graham St, Central; admission free; Ⓜ Central

On the lower reaches west of the 800m-long Central Escalator, the market stalls and open-air canteens centred on Graham St are a compelling destination to stroll around to get a close look at the exotic produce that Hong Kong prides itself in selling and consuming. Preserved 'thousand year' eggs and fresh tofu curd scooped from wooden tubs are just some of the items on display. It's not for the squeamish; fish are cut lengthwise, hearts still beating, for display on the slab. See also p12.

🛍 SHOP

🔲 ADDICTION
回味茶餐廳 Homewares
☎ 2581 2779; 15 Gough St, Central; 🕒 9.30am-6.30pm; Ⓜ Central

Ever more independent retailers are opening up in this corner of

Exquisite wares create a sublime aesthetic – and tempting purchase potential – at Arch Angel Antiques

Soho, and this one sells quirky and endearing design interpretations of everything from lamps to cushions to T-shirts, most of them portable enough to consider buying and taking home.

AMOURS ANTIQUES
Antiques, Clothing

☎ 2803 7877; 45 Staunton St, Soho; ⏲ noon-9pm Mon-Sat, noon-7pm Sun; 🚌 26

This wonderful shop stocks rhinestone jewellery, frocks, and a darling clutch of beaded and tapestry bags dating back to the early 20th century.

ARCH ANGEL ANTIQUES
Antiques, Fine Art

☎ 2851 6848; www.archangel galleries.com; 53-55 Hollywood Rd, Central; ⏲ 9.30am-6.30pm; 🚌 26

Though its specialities are ancient porcelain and tomb ware, Arch Angel packs a lot more into its three floors: everything from mahjong sets and terracotta horses to palatial furniture. It also runs an art gallery, **Arch Angel Contemporary Art** (☎ 2851 6882; 58 Hollywood Rd, Central; ⏲ 9.30am-6.30pm), which is across the road and deals in fine art.

CHINE GALLERY 華
Antiques
☎ 2543 0023; www.chinegallery.com;
42A Hollywood Rd, Soho; ⏱ 10am-6pm
Mon-Sat, 1-6pm Sun; 🚌 13, 26, 40M
This delightful shop sells carefully
restored furniture (we love the
lacquered cabinets) from all over
China and hand-knotted rugs from
remote regions, such as Xinjiang,
Ningxia, Gansu, Inner Mongolia
and Tibet.

EU YAN SANG 余仁生
Medicine
☎ 2544 3870; www.euyansang.com;
152-156 Queen's Rd Central, Soho;
⏱ 9am-7.30pm; M Central
Eu Yan Sang, with branches
throughout Hong Kong, is the
town's most famous dispenser of
traditional Chinese medicines, and
the staff speak good English. It's
also an interesting place to browse
as many of the healing ingredients
are displayed and explained.

GROTTO FINE ART
嘉圖現代藝術有限公司
Fine Art
☎ 2121 2270; www.grottofineart
.com; 2nd fl, 31C-D Wyndham St, Central;
⏱ 11am-7pm Mon-Sat
This small but exquisite gallery
represents predominantly Hong
Kong artists whose work covers
everything from painting and
sculpture to mixed media.

H&M *Clothing & Accessories*
☎ 2110 9546; 68 Queen's Rd Central,
Central; ⏱ 10.30am-8pm Mon-Sat,
11am-8pm Sun; M Central
This Swedish chain has finally
brought its inexpensive, of-the-
moment clothing to Hong Kong.
The appeal is discount prices with
lines that track high-end fashion
trends closely, partly with the help
of collaborations with the likes of
Madonna, Stella McCartney and
Kylie Minogue.

HOBBS & BISHOPS FINE
ART 藝之
Antiques
☎ 2537 9838; 28 Hollywood Rd,
Soho; ⏱ 10am-5.30pm Mon-Sat;
🚌 13, 26, 40M
This shop smells of beeswax and
specialises in lacquered Chinese
wooden furniture from the 19th
and early 20th centuries. The buy-
er's taste leans towards the sleekly
handsome rather than the glitzy.

JILIAN, LINGERIE ON
WYNDHAM
Clothing & Accessories
☎ 2826 9295; Ground fl, 31 Wyndham
St, Central;
Swimwear and lingerie from gos-
samer delicates small enough to
swallow with a glass of water to
rather outré corsetry with strings
and stays and such. There's even a
select range of men's smalls if you

just can't put up with your man's industrial-sized underpants any more.

☐ KARIN WEBER ANTIQUES
Antiques, Fine Art

☎ 2544 5004; www.karinwebergallery .com; 20 Aberdeen St, Soho; 🕙 11am-7pm Mon-Sat; 🚌 26

Karin Weber has a good mix of Chinese country antiques and contemporary Asian artworks. She gives short and useful lectures on antiques and the scene in Hong Kong.

☐ LINVA TAILOR
年華時裝公司
Clothing & Accessories

☎ 2544 2456; 38 Cochrane St, Central; 🕙 9.30am-6.30pm Mon-Sat; 🚌 13, 40M

This is the place to come to buy or have your own cheongsam (see boxed text, p48) stitched up. Bring your own silk or choose from Mr Leung's selection.

☐ MIR ORIENTAL CARPETS
Carpets

☎ 2521 5641; Ground fl, New India House, 52 Wyndham St, Central; 🕙 10am-6.30pm Mon-Sat, 11am-5pm Sun; 🚌 13, 26, 40M

One of Hong Kong's largest stockists of fine rugs, with thousands of carpets from around the world flying in and out of its shop. It's Hong Kong's top specialist for

Persian carpets, both traditional and modern.

☐ MOUNTAIN FOLKCRAFT
高山民藝 *Gifts & Souvenirs*

☎ 2523 2817; 12 Wo On Lane, Central; 🕙 9.30am-6.30pm Mon-Sat; Ⓜ Central

One of the nicest shops in town for folk crafts. There's batik, clothing, woodcarvings and lacquerware made by Chinese and other Asian ethnic minorities. Shop attendants are friendly, and prices reasonable.

☐ PEDDER RED
Shoes, Accessories

☎ 2118 3712; 64-66 Wellington St, Central; 🕙 10am-6.30pm; Ⓜ Central

This is the flagship for a small local chain On Pedder specialising in its own and other famous-brand shoes and accessories for women. Perhaps the best for shoes in Hong Kong.

☐ PHOTO SCIENTIFIC
攝影科學
Photographic Equipment

☎ 2525 0550; Ground fl, Eurasia Bldg, 6 Stanley St, Central; 🕙 9am-7pm Mon-Sat; Ⓜ Central

This shop is the favourite of Hong Kong's professional photographers. You may find cheaper equipment elsewhere, but Photo Scientific has a rock-solid reputation, with labelled prices and no bargaining.

🖥 PLUM BLOSSOMS 萬玉堂
Fine Art

☎ 2521 2189; www.plumblossoms.com; Ground fl, Chinachem Hollywood Centre, 1 Hollywood Rd, Central; ⏱ 10am-6.30pm Mon-Sat; Ⓜ Central (exit D2) 🚌 26

The gallery where the late Rudolf Nureyev used to buy his baubles (and other celebrities continue to do so) is one of the most interesting and well established in Hong Kong.

🖥 RANEE K 郭翠華 *Clothing*
☎ 2108 4068; 16K Gough St, Central; ⏱ 10am-6.30pm; Ⓜ Central

Young local designer Ranee K is a rising star for her combinations of dramatic prints and textures, as well as for her deft adoption of the cuts and styles from both the East and West in her evening and ready-to-wear lines.

🖥 ROCK CANDY *Jewellery*
☎ 2549 1018; www.rockcandy.hk; 1 Elgin St, Soho; ⏱ 11am-8pm Mon-Sat; 🚌 26

Made from black glass and with pin-prick lights illuminating display cases, this goth-glam jewellery shop (and its ubertrendy gewgaws) has to be seen to be believed.

🖥 SELECT 18 *Clothing*
☎ 2545 9932; 57-59 Hollywood Rd, Central; ⏱ 10am-6pm; Ⓜ Central

Definitely worth a look for a small, well-selected range of vintage wear that need not take too much of a rummage.

🖥 TAI YIP ART BOOK CENTRE 大業 *Books*
☎ 2524 5963; www.taiyipart.com .hk; Room 101-102, 1st fl, Capitol Plaza, 2-10 Lyndhurst Tce, Central; ⏱ 10am-7pm Mon-Fri, 10am-6.30pm Sat & Sun; Ⓜ Central

Tai Yip has a terrific selection of books about anything that is Chinese and arty: calligraphy, jade, bronze, costumes, architecture, symbolism. There are outlets in several of Hong Kong's museums, including the Hong Kong Museum of Art (p108).

🖥 WAH TUNG CERAMIC ARTS 華通陶瓷 *Gifts & Souvenirs*
☎ 2543 2823; www.wahtungchina.com; 59 Hollywood Rd, Central; ⏱ 10am-7pm; 🚌 26

The world's largest supplier of hand-decorated ceramics, Wah Tung has everything from brightly painted vases and ginger jars to reproduction Tang dynasty figurines. And what you don't see, staff will source for you.

🖥 WATTIS FINE ART *Antiques*
☎ 2524 5302; www.wattis.com.hk; 2nd fl, 20 Hollywood Rd, Soho; ⏱ 10am-6pm Tue-Sat, 1-5pm Sun; 🚌 26

No place in Hong Kong has a better collection of antique maps for sale than this place; the selection of old photographs of Hong Kong and Macau is also very impressive. Enter from Old Bailey St.

🍴 EAT

🍴 ARCHIE B'S NEW YORK DELI
American Deli $

☎ 2522 1239; Lower ground fl, 7-9 Staunton St, Soho; hotdogs & burgers $35-100, salads $30-50; ⏱ 11am-11pm; Ⓜ Central

This little eatery just off the Central Escalator serves as authentic East Coast American delicatessen food as you'll find west of the US of A. It's pretty much an eat-and-run kind of place, but the few tables in the small alleyway just off Staunton St may have you lingering over your kosher dill pickle or Dr Brown's Cream Soda.

🍴 BRICOLAGE 62 *French* $$$
☎ 2542 1992; 62 Hollywood Rd, Central; ⏱ noon-1am Mon-Sat; Ⓜ Central

Mostly French brasserie-style food cooked from the open kitchen, some great wines and a selection of large (steak frites, braised beef shin) and snack dishes (salt cod cakes, bruschetta) make this tiny place an un-hyped winner.

🍴 CECCONI'S CANTINA
Italian $$$

☎ 2147 5500; 43 Elgin St, Soho; ⏱ noon-3pm & 6.30-10.30pm; Ⓜ Central

The decor may be a bit cold and showroomlike, but the food – such as roasted figs with goats curd, flat pancetta and honey-mustard dressing, and peppered duck and confit leg with sweet potato and lime jus – more than makes up for it.

🍴 CHEZ PATRICK
French $$$

☎ 2541 1401; 26 Peel St, Central; ⏱ noon-3pm & 6.30-10.30pm; Ⓜ Central

This very stylish and very French place is doing so well it has opened up a very smart branch on Sun St in Wan Chai, but we think the authenticity of the French fare here has edge. Great value set lunches.

🍴 CHILLI FAGARA
Sichuanese $$

☎ 2893 3330; Shop E, ground fl, 45-53 Graham St, Soho; ⏱ 11.30am-2.30pm & 5-11.30pm; Ⓜ Central

This new hole-in-the-wall in Soho serves reasonably authentic Sichuan fare and is a welcome addition to the short list of quality local eateries open in this part of Central. Make sure you try all three

MIND YOUR TABLE MANNERS

Dining in Hong Kong is an all-in affair: everyone shares dishes, chats loudly and makes a mess. Food is to be enjoyed whole-heartedly, not picked at discreetly. There are, however, a few points of etiquette it doesn't hurt to know about.

> Wait for others to start before digging in (though as a guest you may be encouraged to start).
> Say thank you if someone puts food into your bowl – this is a courteous gesture.
> Cover your mouth with your hand when using a toothpick.
> Don't try to clean up dishes and detritus – a stained tablecloth is a sign of a good meal.
> Don't be afraid to ask for a fork if you can't manage chopsticks (most Chinese restaurants have them).
> Don't stick chopsticks upright into rice as they can look like incense sticks in a bowl of ashes – a sign of death.
> Don't flip a fish over to reach the flesh on the bottom as the next fishing boat you pass will capsize.

Sichuan tastes: *màa* (spicy), *laat* (hot) and *táam* (mild).

🍴 DA PING HUO 大平伙
Sichuanese $$
☎ 2559 1317, 9051 4496; Lower ground fl, 49 Hollywood Rd, Central; 🕑 6pm-midnight; 🚌 26

Fiery Sichuanese fare is the mouthwatering theme here (including stewed bean curd with minced pork and chilli, or sautéed diced chicken and peanuts in sweet chilli). When she's finished cooking for you, chef Wong Sui-king will sing Chinese opera for you.

🍴 DUKE'S BURGER
American $$
☎ 2526 7062; 5 Staunton St, Soho; 🕑 noon-11pm; Ⓜ Central

Hong Kong has gone totally mad for burgers recently and this place does very posh ones, with Wagyu beef and foie gras for instance, accompanied by all manner of fancy fries.

🍴 FINDS
Scandinavian $$$
☎ 2522 9318; 2nd fl, Lan Kwai Fong Tower, 33 Wyndham St, Central; 🕑 noon-2.30pm & 7-11pm; 🚌 13, 26, 40M

This wonderful place, whose name is an acronym for all the Nordic countries, serves light and very tasty Scandinavian food. The surrounds – faux igloo walls, icicle-dripping chandelier, lots of blue tones – is a cool oasis. There's a gay happy hour called Ice on the first Wednesday of each month (6.30pm to 9pm).

🍴 GOOD LUCK THAI FOOD
好運泰國菜 *Thai* $

☎ 2877 2971; 13 Wing Wah Lane, Lan Kwai Fong; 🕙 11am-2am Mon-Sat, 4pm-midnight Sun; Ⓜ Central

After sinking a few beers in Lan Kwai Fong, make your way over to this chaotic but friendly place at the slops end of the charmingly nicknamed 'Rat Alley' for a cheap fix of late-night Thai and Malay food.

🍴 LIFE *Vegetarian* $

☎ 2810 9777; 10 Shelley St, Soho; 🕙 noon-midnight Mon-Fri, 10am-midnight Sat & Sun; 🚌 26; Ⓥ

Life is a vegetarian's dream come true, serving vegan food and dishes free of gluten, wheat, onion and garlic. Nonvegetarians note – this is tasty stuff. There's a delicatessen and shop (8am to 10.30pm Monday to Friday, 9am to 10.30pm Saturday and Sunday) on the ground floor, a café on the 1st floor and seating up in the rooftop garden.

🍴 LIN HEUNG TEA HOUSE
蓮香樓 *Cantonese* $

☎ 2544 4556; 160-164 Wellington St, Central; 🕙 6am-11pm; Ⓜ Central

This older-style Cantonese restaurant is worth a visit for the tableau: old men reading the newspaper, extended families chatting and large office groups

A vegetarian's paradise – tasty, healthy, meat-free treats are the catch of the day at Life

BUDGET BITES

Familiar Western fast-food chains are everywhere, but if you want a quick fix of something slightly more exotic, try the following local fast-food chains. They are all pretty cheap – about $20 to $65 a meal – and branches are everywhere, but especially in large shopping malls and near MTR stations. Wait for others to start before digging in (though as a guest you may be encouraged to start).

Genki Sushi (www.genkisushi.com.sg) Cheap but tasty Japanese fare.
Maxim's (www.maxims.com.hk) A huge range of Canto dishes.
Mix (www.mix-world.com) Excellent smoothies, wraps, salads and free internet.
Oliver's (www.olivers-supersandwiches.com) Sandwiches and salads.
Saint's Alp Teahouse (www.saints-alp.com.hk) Fantastical tea concoctions (taro green milk tea with tapioca pearls anyone?) and bite-sized snacks.

noshing. There's decent dim sum served from trolleys, so it's good for a late bite or those eating alone.

🍴 LUK YU TEA HOUSE
陸羽茶室 *Dim Sum* $$
☎ 2523 5464; 24-26 Stanley St, Central; ⏱ 7am-10pm; Ⓜ Central
This old-style teahouse is a museum piece in more ways than one. Most of the staff have been here since the early Ming dynasty and are as grumpy as an emperor deposed. Still it's *the* place for tasty dim sum (7am to 5pm) in atmospheric surrounds.

🍴 M AT THE FRINGE
International $$$
☎ 2877 4000; 1st fl, Fringe Club, Dairy Farm Bldg, 2 Lower Albert Rd, Central; ⏱ noon-2.30pm & 7-10.30pm Mon-Fri, 7-10.30pm Sat & Sun; Ⓜ Central

No one seems to have a bad thing to say about Michelle's. The menu changes constantly, and everything is consistently excellent, be it crab soufflé, the foie gras two ways or the famous slow-baked salted lamb. It's definitely worth saving room for the splendid desserts.

🍴 MAK'S NOODLE
麥奀雲吞麵世家
Cantonese $
☎ 2854 3810; 77 Wellington St, Central; dishes $25-50; ⏱ 11am-8pm; Ⓜ Central, then bus 40M westbound from Wan Chai Ferry or Pacific Place, Admiralty
This noodle shop sells excellent wonton soup, and the beef brisket noodles, more of a Western taste than a Chinese one, are highly recommended. Go for lunch or eat early; it's shut tight by 8pm.

🍴 NHA TRANG 芽莊
Vietnamese $

☎ 2581 9992; 88 Wellington St, Central; 🕙 noon-11pm; Ⓜ Central

The regular Vietnamese clientele at this simple but stylish restaurant is testament to the quality and authenticity of the food.

🍴 SHUI HU JU 水滸居
Sichuanese $$

☎ 2869 6927; 68 Peel St, Soho; 🕙 6pm-midnight; 🚌 26

This restaurant serves earthy, chilli-packed Sichuanese dishes (at dinner only) in a delightful Chinese setting that feels like you're dining in one of the neighbouring antiques shops.

🍴 YUN FU 雲府
Northern Chinese $$$

☎ 2116 8855; Basement, Yu Yuet Lai Bldg, 43-45 Wyndham St, Central; Ⓜ Central

BOOKING & TIPPING
It's advisable to book ahead in all but the cheapest restaurants, especially on Friday and Saturday nights. Most restaurants add a 10% service charge to the bill. If the service at a top-end restaurant was outstanding, you might consider adding another 5% or 10% on top of the service charge. At cheap or midrange places, a couple of coins is sufficient.

There's a *Crouching Tiger, Hidden Dragon* feel to this fantastical place. After an exotic cocktail garnished with dry seahorses or lizards, try the goose liver soaked in dark soy sauce, the sliced duck fillet wrapped in tofu paper or the whole roasted bamboo shoot served in its bark.

🍴 YUNG KEE 鏞記酒家
Cantonese $$$

☎ 2522 1624; 32-40 Wellington St, Central; 🕙 11am-11.30pm; Ⓜ Central (exit D2)

This long-standing institution is probably the most famous Cantonese restaurant in Hong Kong. Yung Kee's roast goose has been the talk of the town since 1942, and its dim sum (2pm to 5.30pm Monday to Saturday, 11am to 5.30pm Sunday) is excellent.

🍸 DRINK

🍸 2121 2121酒吧 *Bar*

☎ 2804 6669; Ground fl, The Plaza, 21 D'Aguilar St, Lan Kwai Fong; 🕙 4pm-1am Mon-Thu, 4pm-4am Fri-Sat, Sun 6-9pm, happy hr 4-9pm; Ⓜ Central

Right in the heart of the 'Fong but when we last visited somehow managing not to be part of the general crush, this is a small but elegant bar overlooking the street action, with a DJ, cocktails and wine.

Low-key with a chilled vibe – the ambient interior of Bar 1911 is an inviting proposition

⅋ BAR 1911 *Bar*

☎ 2810 6681; 7 Staunton St, Soho;
🕑 5pm-midnight Mon-Sat, happy hr
5-9pm; Ⓜ Central
This is a very refined bar with
fine details (stained glass, ceiling
fans, lanterns), a 1920s vibe and a
relaxed atmosphere.

⅋ BARCO *Wine Bar*

☎ 2857 4478; 42 Staunton St, Soho;
🕑 4pm-1am Sun-Thu, 4pm-late Fri &
Sat, happy hr 4-8pm; Ⓜ Central
One of our favourite Soho bars,
Barco has great staff, is small
enough to never feel empty, and
attracts a cool mix of locals and
expats.

⅋ CLUB 71 *Bar*

☎ 2858 7071; Basement, 67 Hollywood
Rd, Central; 🕑 3pm-2am Mon-Sat, 6pm-
1am Sun, happy hr 3-9pm; 🚌 26
When Club 64, the counter-
culture nerve centre of Lan Kwai
Fong (a name recalling the 4 June
1989 Tiananmen Square massacre
in Beijing), was forced to close,
some of the owners relocated to
this alley north of Hollywood Rd.
Named after the huge protest
march held on 1 July 2003, Club
71 is again one of the best drinking spots for nonposeurs. Get to it
via a small footpath running west
off Peel St.

☿ CLUB FEATHER BOA *Bar*

☎ 2857 2586; 38 Staunton St, Soho; ⏲ 8pm-late Tue-Sat; Ⓜ Central
Feather Boa is a plush lounge hidden behind gold drapes. Part camp lounge, part bordello – part those curtains and get stuck into one of its infamous mango daiquiris.

☿ DRAGON-I *Bar*

☎ 3110 1222; Upper ground fl, The Centrium, 60 Wyndham St, Central; ⏲ noon-midnight Mon-Sat, happy hr 5-9pm; Ⓜ Central
This delightful venue on the edge of Soho has both an indoor bar and restaurant and a huge terrace overlooking Wyndham St filled with caged songbirds. You'd *almost* think you were in the country.

HAPPY HOUR

During certain hours of the day, most pubs, bars and even some clubs give discounts on drinks (usually one-third to one-half off) or offer a two-for-one deal. Happy hour is usually in the late afternoon or early evening (eg 4pm to 8pm) but the times vary widely from place to place. Depending on the season, the day of the week and the location, some pub happy hours run from midday till as late as 10pm, and some resume after midnight for an hour or so.

☿ GECKO LOUNGE
Bar, Live Music

☎ 2537 4680; Lower ground fl, 15-19 Hollywood Rd, Central; ⏲ 4pm-3am Mon-Thu, 4pm-6am Fri & Sat, happy hr 6-9pm; Ⓜ Central
Gecko is a relaxed hideout that attracts a fun crowd, especially to its live jazz sessions Tuesday to Thursday. The well-hidden DJ mixes good grooves with kooky Parisian tunes on weekends. There's a great wine list. Enter from Ezra's Lane off Cochrane or Pottinger Sts.

☿ PEAK CAFE BAR 山頂餐廳
Bar, Café

☎ 2140 6877; 9-13 Shelley St, Soho; ⏲ 11am-2am Mon-Sat, 11am-midnight Sun, happy hr 5-8pm; 🚌 13, 26, 40M
The fixtures and fittings of the much-missed Peak Cafe, from 1947, have moved down the hill to this comfy bar with super cocktails and excellent nosh. The only thing missing is the view.

☿ SODA *Bar*

☎ 2522 8118; Upper basement, 79 Wyndham St, Central; ⏲ 4pm-midnight Sun-Thu, 4pm-3am Fri & Sat, happy hr 6-9pm; 🚌 13, 26, 40M
This well-placed watering hole, decorated in warm yellows and oranges, and with its front open to steep Pottinger St, is also a DJ scene, notably on Wednesday and

Soaking up the Soho atmosphere at Staunton's Wine Bar & Cafe

the weekend, with hip-hop and R 'n' B. Enter from Pottinger St.

☕ SOLAS *Bar*
☎ 9154 4049; www.solas.com.hk; 60 Wyndham St, Central; ⏰ noon-2am Mon-Sat; Ⓜ Central
If the nasty man wouldn't let you into Dragon-I upstairs, never mind. This relaxed, friendly place, where a DJ spins chilled lounge sounds and the cocktails pack a punch, isn't a bad consolation prize.

☕ STAUNTON'S WINE BAR & CAFÉ *Bar, Café*
☎ 2973 6611; 10-12 Staunton St, Soho; ⏰ 8.30am-2am midnight, happy hr 5-9pm; 🚌 13, 12, 26
Staunton's is swish, cool and on the ball, with decent wine and a lovely terrace. For eats, there's light fare downstairs and a modern international restaurant called Scirocco above.

☕ TIVO *Bar*
☎ 2116 8055; www.aqua.com.hk; 43-55 Wyndham St, Central; ⏰ noon-2am Mon-Sat; Ⓜ Central
One of the best of a lively little string of bars that have sprung up here, sophisticated Tivo is a cut above the nuts and beer standard of the 'Fong, just around the corner. Italian aperitivo-type snacks are available to wash down the wine or cocktails.

⭐ PLAY

✴ CALIFORNIA
Club, Live Music
☎ 2521 1345; Ground fl, California Tower, 30-32 D'Aguilar St, Lan Kwai Fong; ⏰ 6pm-3am Mon-Fri, 9pm-late Sat, happy hr 6-9pm Mon-Fri; Ⓜ Central
This revamped Lan Kwai Fong stalwart has been recast as a rather masculine space with leather banquettes and smoked mirrors. There's live music, funk or jazz from Thursday to Saturday. The rest of the week it's all about the food.

✴ CAVERN *Live Music*
☎ 2121 8969; Shop 1, lower ground fl, Lan Kwai Fong Tower, 33 Wyndham St, Lan Kwai Fong; ⏰ 5pm-2am, happy hr 5-9pm; Ⓜ Central
Don't expect this place to break any new ground, or any new acts. The Cavern is a showcase for tribute bands, usually vintage 1960s. Music from 8pm (7.30pm Sunday) is unplugged at 11pm (10.30pm Sunday). Enter from D'Aguilar St.

✴ CLUB 97 *Club*
☎ 2186 1897; Ground fl, Cosmos Bldg, 9-11 Lan Kwai Fong, Lan Kwai Fong ⏰ 6pm-2am Mon-Thu, 6pm-4am Fri, 8pm-4am Sat & Sun, happy hr 6-9pm Mon-Thu & Sat, 6-10pm Fri, 8-10pm Sun; Ⓜ Central
This schmoozy lounge-bar has a popular happy hour (it's a gay

Pumping music, killer cocktails and wall-to-wall revellers – just another night out on the tiles at Drop

event on Friday night) and there's salsa on Wednesday. Club 97 has a 'members only' policy to turn away the underdressed, so make an effort.

⭐ DROP *Club*
☎ 2543 8856, 2543 9230; Basement, On Lok Mansion, 39-43 Hollywood Rd, Central; ☽ 7pm-2am Tue, to 3am Wed, to 4am Thu, to 5am Fri, 10pm-5am Sat, 9pm-2am Sun, happy hr 7-10pm Tue-Fri; 🚌 13, 26, 40M

Deluxe lounge decor, excellent bleep bleep music, potent cocktails and an up-for-it crowd keep Drop strong on the scene. The members-only policy after 11pm Thursday to Saturday is enforced

to keep the dance-floor capacity at a manageable 'in like sardines' level. Enter from Cochrane St.

⭐ ELEMIS DAY SPA
Health & Fitness
☎ 2521 6660; www.elemisdayspa .com.hk; 9 fl, Century Sq, 1 D'Aguilar St, Central; Ⓜ Central

The Elemis provides luxurious surroundings and utterly soothing treatments without absolutely breaking the bank. Pampering and treatments range from basic facials to deep tissue massage. There are separate sections (and treatment menus) for men and women. Its very central location is another plus.

⭐ FRINGE CLUB, THEATRE & STUDIO 藝穗會
Live Music, Theatre

☎ 2521 7251, theatre bookings 2521 9126; www.hkfringeclub.com; Ground & 1st fl, Fringe Club, Dairy Farm Bldg, 2 Lower Albert Rd, Central; theatre tickets $100-300; ☼ noon-midnight Mon-Thu, noon-3am Fri & Sat, happy hr 3-9pm Mon-Thu, 3-8pm Fri & Sat; Ⓜ Central (exit G)

The Fringe, a friendly and eclectic venue on the border of the Lan Kwai Fong quadrant, has original music in its gallery-bar from 10.30pm on Friday and Saturday, with jazz, rock and world music getting the most airplay. There's a pleasant rooftop bar open in the warmer months. The intimate theatres, each seating up to a hundred, host eclectic local and international performances in English and Cantonese.

⭐ HAPPY FOOT REFLEXOLOGY 知足樂 *Health & Fitness*

☎ 2544 1010; 11th fl & 13th fl, Jade Centre, 98-102 Wellington St, Central; ☼ 10am-midnight; Ⓜ Central

Give your walk-weary tootsies (or other bits and pieces) a pampering at the aptly named Happy Foot. Foot/body massages start at $220 for 50 minutes. A pedicure costs $175.

⭐ HOME *Club*

☎ 2545 0023; 2nd fl, 23 Hollywood Rd, Central; ☼ 10pm-3am Mon-Fri, 10pm-9am Sat, happy hr midnight-3am Wed & Thu; 🚌 13, 26, 40M

A meet 'n' greet and more for the styled and/or beautiful early on, this place turns into a bump 'n' grind later. With chill beds and a bouncy castle floor – well, anything goes. It's still partying well after dawn.

WHAT'S ON WHERE & WHEN

Artslink (www.hkac.org.hk) A monthly with listings of performances, exhibitions and art-house film screenings. Published by the Hong Kong Arts Centre.

bc magazine (www.bcmagazine.net) A free biweekly guide to Hong Kong's entertainment and partying scene.

Cityline (☎ 2314 4228; www.cityline.com.hk) Affiliate of Urbtix; also good for bookings.

hkclubbing.com (www.hkclubbing.com) Especially useful for clubbing and parties.

HK Magazine (www.asia-city.com) A very comprehensive entertainment listings magazine. It's free, appears on Friday, and can be found at restaurants, bars, shops and hotels.

Time Out (www.timeout.com.hk) An authoritative fortnightly guide and listings to what's on.

Urbtix (☎ 2111 5999; www.urbtix.gov.hk) Bookings for most cultural events can be made online or by phone.

Wendy Wen
DJ at Yumla, Central

And you are? A L'Oreal saleswoman by day, a DJ by night at Yumla (opposite). **So what are the kids listening to at the moment?** Minimal techno, sparse beats and hip-hop are big in Hong Kong right now. Progressive house is still going pretty strong and Cantopop's still popular. **What's the top spot to go for a good night out?** Yumla, of course. It's the best club in Hong Kong, but I'm biased as I play there. It's always good, though, and the music's always cool. **Where do you go when you're not in a club (or at work)?** I head to the beach, at South Bay around the Repulse Bay (p102) area.

⭐ JOYCE IS NOT HERE
Live Music

☎ 2851 2999; 38-44 Peel St, Soho; ⏰ 11am-late Tue-Fri, 10am-late Sat & Sun, happy hr 4-8pm; 🚌 13, 26, 40M

This super-chilled café-bar in reds, whites and blacks has something for everyone – from poetry readings and live music to Sunday brunch – attracting a good mix of expats and locals. Love the place.

⭐ PROPAGANDA *Club*

☎ 2868 1316; Lower ground fl, 1 Hollywood Rd, Central; admission $20-200 Fri & Sat; ⏰ 9pm-4am Tue-Thu, 9pm-6am Fri & Sat; 🚌 13, 26, 40M

This is Hong Kong's premier gay dance club. Enter from Ezra's Lane, which runs between Pottinger and Cochrane Sts.

⭐ PURE FITNESS *Heath & Fitness*

☎ 2970 3366; www.pure-fit.com; 1st, 2nd & 3rd fl, Kinwick Centre, 32 Hollywood Rd, Soho; ⏰ 6am-midnight Mon-Sat, 8am-10pm Sun; Ⓜ Central

Enter this favourite of the Soho set from Shelley St.

⭐ SENSE OF TOUCH
Health & Fitness

☎ 2526 6918; www.senseoftouch.com.hk; 1st-5th fl, 52 D'Aguilar St, Lan Kwai Fong; ⏰ 11am-midnight Mon-Fri, 10.30am-7pm Sat, 10.30am-7pm Sun; Ⓜ Central

This award-winning spa offers every conceivable form of treatment (cappuccino wrap, anyone?) but most are Asian in origin, including ayurvedic massage ($600 per hour) and Thai hot-poultice therapy. If you're trying to shift that jetlag at a weird hour, there are 'night spa' treatments until midnight.

⭐ YOGA PLUS
Health & Fitness

☎ 2521 4555; www.yogaplus.com.hk; 6th fl, LKF Tower, 55 D'Aguilar St, Central; ⏰ 7am-11pm Mon-Sun; Ⓜ Central

A plush, modern place occupying the same block as Hotel LKF and offering spa treatments, Pilates and 11 styles of yoga, including Hatha, Iyengar and (we promise we're not making this up) 'golf' yoga.

⭐ YUMLA *Club*

☎ 2147 2383; Lower basement, 79 Wyndham St, Central; ⏰ 5pm-2am Mon-Thu, 5pm-4am Fri & Sat, 7pm-2am Sun, happy hr 5-9pm Mon-Sat, 7-9pm Sun; 🚌 13, 26, 40M

This place below chilled Soda (p67) is arguably the hippest and least pretentious club in Hong Kong, with a cool crowd and excellent tunes. Watch out for the murals. The entrance is on Pottinger St.

>HONG KONG ISLAND: THE MID-LEVELS & THE PEAK

Not taking the trip up Hong Kong's Peak (the highest point on the island) is like visiting Paris without ascending the Eiffel Tower. It's on every visitor's list and rightly so. On a clear day (sadly an increasingly rare thing) the views are spectacular but at any time, day or night, the cool breezes and the views down onto the concrete canyons are wonderful. The 3km walk around the base of the Peak's summit presents a shaded panoramic view of harbour, city and sea. The Peak is also one of the best places to dine with a view, and it's a jumping-off point for the Hong Kong Trail. To get there board the hair-raisingly steep Peak Tram and perhaps on the way back down take a taxi or bus to do some billionaire's mansion spotting. The Mid-Levels, halfway up the Peak, is solidly residential and has relatively little to offer tourists in the way of sights, though there are a few gems.

THE MID-LEVELS & THE PEAK

Park Rd

(A) (B) (C) (D)

Blake
Garden

Bonham Rd

Breezy Path

See Central &
Sheung Wan
Map p41

1

Lyttelton Rd

To Hing Hong Kui In Fong Sq St

St Hollywood Rd

Caine La

Shing Wong

Wing Lee St

SOHO

Kotewall Rd

Seymour Rd

Staunton St

THE MID-LEVELS

Castle Rd

C 3

Aberdeen St

C 7

Caine Rd

2

Po Shan Rd

Conduit Rd

Robinson Rd

St Leung Fai Terr

Shelley St

8 🏛 **2**

Mosque St

Mosque Jct

Hornsey Rd

3

Mt Austin Rd

▲ **Victoria
Peak**
(552m)

Lugard Rd

**Pok Fu Lam
Country
Park**

4

May Rd

Mt Austin Rd

5

Governor's Walk

THE PEAK

Tregunter Path

Old Peak Rd

6

Harlech Rd

Peak Rd

Finlay Rd

5
🏛 ● *Peak Tower*

6 🏛

4

*Peak Tram
Terminus*

Tramway

0   200 m
0   0.1 miles

LP

👁 SEE

👁 DR SUN YAT SEN MUSEUM
孫中山紀念館
☎ 2367 6373; www.lcsd.gov.hk/CE/Museum/sysm; 7 Castle Rd, Mid-Levels; adult/child, student or senior over 60 $10/5, free after 2pm Tue; ⏰ 10am-6pm Mon-Wed & Fri & Sat, 10am-7pm Sun; 🚌 3B, alight at the Hong Kong Baptist Church on Caine Rd

A hugely significant historical figure, Dr Sun Yat Sen was an early 20th-century revolutionary dedicated to overthrowing the Qing dynasty. Educated in Hong Kong, his experience of the colony and the efficient manner in which it was run was one of the formative experiences that put him on the path to revolution. His story is one of the more interesting chapters in Hong Kong and China's history, so it's certainly worth a visit. Audioguides cost $10.

👁 HONG KONG MUSEUM OF MEDICAL SCIENCES
香港醫學博物館
☎ 2549 5123; www.hkmms.org.hk; 2 Caine Lane, Mid-Levels; adult/child $10/5; ⏰ 10am-5pm Tue-Sat, 1-5pm Sun; 🚌 3B, 23, 23B, 40, 40M, 103, green minibus 8 (from GPO)

This small museum of medical implements and accoutrements is less interesting for its exhibits than for its architecture and attached herb garden. It occupies what was once the Old Pathological

Institute, an Edwardian-style brick-and-tile structure built in 1905. The exhibits comparing Chinese and Western approaches to medicine are unusual and instructive.

👁 OHEL LEAH SYNAGOGUE
☎ 2589 2621; www.ohelleah.org; 70 Robinson Rd, Mid-Levels; admission free; ⏰ 10.30am-7pm Mon-Thu; 🚌 3B, 13, 23, 23B, 40

This 'Moorish Romantic' temple, completed in 1902, is named after Leah Gubbay Sassoon, matriarch of a wealthy (and philanthropic) Sephardic Jewish family that can trace its roots back to the beginning of the colony. Bring your passport and expect a thorough security check if you plan to visit the sumptuous interior.

🍴 EAT

🍴 CAFE DECO
International $$$
☎ 2849 5111; Levels 1 & 2, Peak Galleria, 118 Peak Rd, The Peak; ⏰ 11.30am-midnight Mon-Thu, 11.30am-1am Fri & Sat, 9.30am-midnight Sun; 🚡 Peak Tram 🚌 15; ♿

Most punters would be content with the views, live jazz (7pm to 11pm Thursday to Saturday) and stylish art-deco furnishings. But the eclectic menu – offering everything from the simple but fresh (oysters, sushi) to more complex bistro and Indian dishes – is way above

TRAM BEATS SEDAN

In 1885 everyone thought that Phineas Kyrie and William Kerfoot Hughes were crazy when they announced their intention to build a funicular tram to the top of Victoria Peak, but it opened successfully three years later, wiping out the lucrative sedan-chair trade almost overnight. Since then the tram has never had an accident and has been stopped only by WWII and the violent rainstorms of 1966, which washed half the track down the hill.

average. There's also an excellent weekend brunch (11.30am to 2.30pm).

🍴 EATING PLUS
International, Asian $

☎ 2849 7855; Shop P102, level 1, Peak Tower, 128 Peak Rd, The Peak; ⏱ 11.30am-10pm; 🚃 Peak Tram 🚌 15 Style comes cheap at this voguish, healthy, fast-food joint in the Peak Tower. Omelettes are fluffy, juices freshly squeezed, and lunch and dinner extend to soups, noodles (a successful mix of East and West) and rice dishes, including risotto.

🍴 PEAK LOOKOUT
International, Asian $$$

☎ 2849 1000; 121 Peak Rd, The Peak; ⏱ 10.30am-midnight Mon-Fri, 8.30am-1am Sat, 8.30am-midnight Sun; 🚃 Peak Tram 🚌 15

East meets West at this colonial-style restaurant, serving everything from Indian and French to Thai and Italian in the handsome dark-wood interior and the leafy terrace. Stick to the oysters, the barbecue and the views, which are to the south of the island, not over the harbour. Good breakfasts, too.

🍴 PEARL ON THE PEAK
International, Fusion $$$

☎ 2849 5123, 2101 1268; Level 1, Peak Tower, 128 Peak Rd, The Peak; ⏱ 11.30am-midnight Mon-Fri, 9am-midnight Sat & Sun; 🚃 Peak Tram 🚌 15 Be in no doubt that this is a tourist restaurant, so the food is merely good, the prices are high but the views are great. It's just a shame it doesn't aim higher than the pasta to curry, with twists of Oz, menu. The signature pearl meat (air-freighted) flash fried with shiitake, chives, ginger and soy is an un-ecofriendly exception.

🍴 PHOENIX
International, Modern British $$$

☎ 2546 2110; 29 Shelley St, Mid-Levels; ⏱ 4-11pm Mon-Thu, 11am-11pm Fri, 9am-11pm Sat & Sun; 🚌 12, 13, 23A This little gastropub chalks up its dishes daily depending on what's good and in season. It serves a mix of hearty modern British comfort food and smaller tasting dishes along more Mediterranean lines. It's a great place for weekend brunch (9am to 4pm).

HONG KONG ISLAND: ADMIRALTY & WAN CHAI

>HONG KONG ISLAND: ADMIRALTY & WAN CHAI

Things are changing for the better in Wan Chai. The cheap canteen-style eating places, a dozen or so seedy hostess bars and a clutch of expat watering holes between Gloucester and Hennessy Rds are all much the same as ever. But head inland and you'll find a new side to Wan Chai. Just east of the Pacific Place mall and south of the tram tracks, you'll find great little restaurants, bars and boutiques sharing space with traditional shops, markets and workshops. On the other side of Pacific Place in Admiralty there are a few buildings of note amid a slightly confusing and disjointed tangle of bridges and underpasses. They include the blindingly gold Far East Finance Centre, known locally as 'Amah's Tooth', a reference to the traditional Chinese maids' preference for gold fillings and caps. Closer to the water the sweeping curves, striking setting and acres of glass make the Hong Kong Convention and Exhibition Centre well worth further investigation.

ADMIRALTY & WAN CHAI

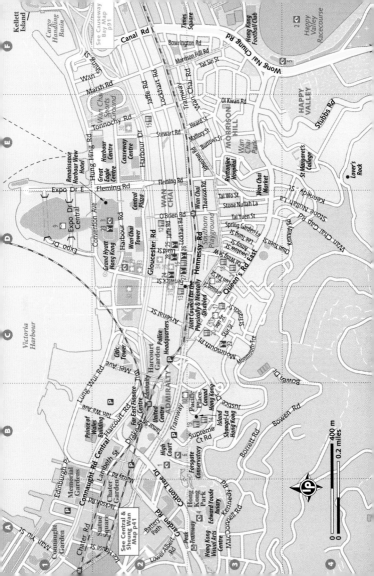

◉ SEE

◉ HONG KONG CONVENTION & EXHIBITION CENTRE
香港會議展覽中心

☎ 2582 8888; www.hkcec.com; 1 Expo Dr, Wan Chai; admission free; 🚌 18 Ⓜ Wan Chai

This enormous complex, built in 1988 and extended onto reclaimed land for the handover ceremony in 1997, boasts an enormous 'glass curtain' – a window seven storeys high – facing the harbour. On the waterfront promenade to the northeast is the Golden Bauhinia, a 6m-tall statue of Hong Kong's symbol marking the establishment of the Hong Kong Special Administrative Region (SAR).

◉ HONG KONG PARK
香港公園

☎ 2521 5041; www.lcsd.gov.hk/parks/hkp/en/index.php; 19 Cotton Tree Dr, Admiralty; admission free; 🕐 park 6am-11pm, conservatory & aviary 9am-5pm, tours 8-10am Wed; 🚌 12A Ⓜ Admiralty (exit C1) 🚻

We like to visit the park primarily to walk among our fine-feathered friends at their level (p24), but there are a couple of other drawcards here, including the **Flagstaff House Museum of Tea Ware** (☎ 2869 0690; www.lcsd.gov.hk/CE/Museum/Arts/english/tea/intro/eintro.html; 10 Cotton Tree Dr, Admiralty; admission free; 🕐 10am-5pm

Wed-Mon) housed in the oldest colonial building (1846) extant in Hong Kong. It contains a collection of antique Chinese tea ware. Next door the **KS Lo Gallery** (🕐 10am-5pm Wed-Mon) contains rare Chinese ceramics and stone seals collected by the gallery's eponymous benefactor. There is also a squash and sports centre for those inclined.

◉ PAO GALLERIES 包氏畫廊

☎ 2824 5330; www.hkac.org.hk; 2 Harbour Rd, Wan Chai; admission free; 🕐 during exhibitions 10am-6pm; 🚌 12 Ⓜ Wan Chai (exit A1)

This major contemporary art gallery in the Hong Kong Arts Centre (p89) hosts retrospectives and group shows in all visual media. The curatorial vision is lively without being too provocative. After all, this is Hong Kong.

LOST HERITAGE

Hong Kong's dreadful track record when it comes to preserving old buildings persists to this day. Land is scarce and valuable, heritage laws are minimal and developers have power. The latest building under threat is Wan Chai's handsome old art-deco market (in distinctive Streamline Moderne style), located near Wan Chai Park. Heritage campaigners are clamouring for its preservation, but having lost the historic and iconic Hong Kong Island ferry piers to land reclamation a few years back, no one's counting on anything.

SHOP

COSMOS BOOKS 天地圖書
Books

☎ 2866 1677; Basement & 1st fl, 30 Johnston Rd, Wan Chai; ☺ 10am-8pm; Ⓜ Wan Chai (exit A3) ⓘ

This outlet has a good selection of China-related books in its basement. Upstairs there are English-language books (a large selection of nonfiction) plus one of the city's best stationery departments.

DESIGN GALLERY
Gifts & Souvenirs

☎ 2584 4146; www.hkdesigngallery.com; Hong Kong Convention & Exhibition Centre, 1 Harbour Rd, Wan Chai; ☺ 10am-7.30pm Mon-Fri, 10am-7pm Sat, noon-7.30pm Sun; 🚌 18 Ⓜ Wan Chai

Supported by the Hong Kong Trade Development Council, this shop showcases Hong Kong design in the form of jewellery, toys, ornaments and gadgets. It's a somewhat chaotic – but often rewarding – gaggle of goodies.

HONG KONG RECORDS
香港唱片 *Music*

☎ 2845 7088, 2530 9696; Shop 253, 2nd fl, Pacific Place, 88 Queensway, Admiralty; ☺ 10am-8.30pm Mon-Thu, 10am-9pm Fri-Sun; Ⓜ Admiralty ⓘ

If you're looking for something different, this outfit has a good

Hong Kong Convention & Exhibition Centre

selection of local and international sounds, including traditional Chinese, jazz, classical and contemporary music. It also offers a good range of both Chinese and Western (with Chinese subtitles) film DVDs. Make sure they work for your DVD region.

KELLY & WALSH *Books*

☎ 2522 5743; www.kellyandwalsh.com; Shop 236, 2nd fl, Pacific Place, 88 Queensway, Admiralty; ☺ 10.30am-8pm Sun-Thu, 10.30am-8.30pm Fri & Sat; Ⓜ Admiralty ⓘ

This smart shop has a great choice of art, design and culinary books, and the staff know the stock well.

The children's books are shelved in a handy kids' reading lounge.

KENT & CURWEN
Clothing & Accessories

☎ 2840 0023; Shop 224, 2nd fl, Pacific Place, 88 Queensway, Admiralty; ⏱ 10am-8pm Sun-Thu, 10am-9pm Fri & Sat; Ⓜ Admiralty 🚇

Distinguished suits, dress shirts, ties, cufflinks and casual tops for the gentleman who'd rather look to the manor born than arriviste broke.

PACIFIC CUSTOM TAILORS
Clothing & Accessories

☎ 2845 5377; Shop 113, 1st fl, Pacific Place, 88 Queensway, Admiralty; ⏱ 9.30am-7.30pm Mon-Sat; Ⓜ Admiralty 🚇

This is our favourite bespoke tailor in Hong Kong, wrapping us in new duds many times. Staff will make or copy anything; turnaround on most items is two or three days, including two fittings. Excellent, personable service.

SONJIA
Clothing, Homewares

☎ 2529 6223; 2 Sun St, Wan Chai; ⏱ 9.30am-7.30pm Mon-Sat; Ⓜ Admiralty 🚇

Sumptuous, romantic womenswear creations from this Anglo-Korean Hong Kong designer in silk, velvet and fine cotton, much of it hand finished with embroidery, plus vintage jewellery and a few international labels, such as Lagerfeld. The adjoining store stocks a select bunch of elegant homewares to suit every taste.

VIVIENNE TAM
Clothing & Accessories

☎ 2918 0238; www.viviennetam.com; Shop 209, 1st fl, Pacific Place, 88 Queensway, Admiralty; ⏱ 11am-8.30pm Sun-Thu, 11am-9pm Fri & Sat; Ⓜ Admiralty 🚇

Sophisticated yet adventurous womenswear from New York–based designer Vivienne Tam, who was trained in Hong Kong.

WISE KIDS *Toys*

☎ 2868 0133; www.wisekidstoys.com; Shop 134, 1st fl, Pacific Place, 88 Queensway, Admiralty; ⏱ 10am-8pm Sun-Wed, 10am-9pm Thu-Sat; Ⓜ Admiralty 🚇

SALE ON

Winter sales are held during the first three weeks of January and summer sales in late June and early July. Hong Kong pretties itself up for Fashion Week, the industry's most important annual event, in mid-January (autumn and winter) and mid-July (spring and summer; see the boxed text, p30). The main parades and events take place at the Hong Kong Convention & Exhibition Centre (p80) in Wan Chai, but keep an eye out for shows and shindigs in shopping malls around the territory.

Nothing to plug in and nothing with batteries: Wise Kids concentrates on kids generating energy with what's upstairs. Along with stuffed toys, card games and things to build, there are practical items such as toilet-lid locks and carryalls.

🍴 EAT

The Wan Chai dining scene is changing fast and much for the better. The area around Johnston Rd and Ship St is especially promising with new places popping up all the time.

🍴 369 SHANGHAI RESTAURANT 上海三六九飯店
Shanghainese $$

☎ 2527 2343; 30-32 O'Brien Rd, Wan Chai; ⏰ 11am-4am; Ⓜ Wan Chai

Low-key Shanghainese eatery that's nothing like five-star but does the dumpling job well. It's family run, with good comfy booths in the front window and open late, for stumbling in after a night out on the Wanch. Try its signature hot and sour soup ($40).

🍴 AMERICAN RESTAURANT 美利堅京菜
Northern Chinese $$

☎ 2527 7277; Ground fl, Golden Star Bldg, 20 Lockhart Rd, Wan Chai; ⏰ 11am-11.30pm; Ⓜ Wan Chai

This place, which chose its name to lure American sailors on R&R through its doors during the Vietnam War, has been serving earthy Northern Chinese cuisine for over half a century. As you'd expect, the Peking duck ($275) and the beggar's chicken ($385) are tops.

🍴 CAFÉ TOO
International $$

☎ 2820 8571; 7th fl, Island Shangri-La Hong Kong, Pacific Place, Supreme Court Rd, Admiralty; ⏰ 6.30am-1am; Ⓜ Admiralty

This immensely popular, beautifully designed food hall has a half-dozen kitchens preparing dishes from around the world and one of the best buffets in town. There are à la carte options and lighter fare, such as sandwiches.

🍴 CARRIANNA CHIU CHOW RESTAURANT 佳寧娜潮州菜
Chiu Chow $$$

☎ 2511 1282; 1st fl, AXA Centre, 151 Gloucester Rd, Wan Chai; ⏰ 11am-11.30pm; Ⓜ Wan Chai

For Chiu Chow food, the Carrianna still rates very high after all these years. Try the cold dishes (sliced goose with vinegar, crab claws), pork with tofu or Chiu Chow–style chicken. Enter from Tonnochy Rd.

NEIGHBOURHOODS

HONG KONG ISLAND: ADMIRALTY & WAN CHAI

🍽 CHE'S CANTONESE RESTAURANT 車氏粵菜軒
Cantonese $$$

☎ 2528 1123; 4th fl, Broadway, 54-62 Lockhart Rd, Wan Chai; 🕙 11am-3pm & 6-11.30pm; Ⓜ Wan Chai

This excellent Cantonese restaurant serves many home-style delicacies and offers a special seasonal menu with a dozen additional dishes.

🍽 NATURO+ 天廷食品
Café $$

☎ 2865 0388; 6 Sun St, Wan Chai; 🕙 9am-6pm; Ⓜ Wan Chai

Peaceful outdoor seating and a small range of snacks and sandwiches, plus wonderful cheesecake made from Tibetan yak's milk, make this leafy, secluded Wan Chai wholefood store and café a great spot for lunch. See also opposite.

🍽 PAWN *Gastropub* $$$

☎ 2866 3444; 62 Johnston Rd, Wan Chai; 🕙 11am-late; Ⓜ Wan Chai

Occupying an old colonial-era building with some great terrace dining overlooking the trams, the Pawn serves accomplished modern British pub grub (fish and chips, ham hock and prune salad) and roast pork belly, plus a great list of wines by the glass, carafe or bottle. It's popular, so book ahead.

🍽 PETRUS *French* $$$

☎ 2820 8590; 56th fl, Island Shangri-La Hong Kong, Pacific Place, Supreme Court Rd, Admiralty; 🕙 noon-3pm & 6.30-11pm Mon-Sat; Ⓜ Admiralty

With its head (and prices, it must be said) in the clouds, Petrus is one of the finest restaurants in Hong Kong. Expect traditional (not nouvelle) French cuisine and stunning harbour views. Coat and tie required for guys.

🍽 THAI BASIL *Thai* $$

☎ 2537 4682; Shop 005, lower ground fl, Pacific Place, 88 Queensway, Admiralty; 🕙 11.30am-10.45pm; Ⓜ Admiralty 🚊

This restaurant in a mall basement (did we say mall basement?) turns out some surprisingly authentic (and quite lovely) Thai dishes. This may not be a destination but it's not a bad pit stop while shopping.

🍽 XI YAN SWEETS 囍宴甜藝
Cantonese, Fusion $$

☎ 2866 0868; 18 Ship St, Wan Chai; 🕙 noon-2.30pm & 7-10.30pm Mon-Sat; Ⓜ Wan Chai

The new joint from a local TV chef who runs private dining club Xi Yan serves an oddly successful fusion of Asian savoury dishes (shrimp and pomelo salad, osmanthus smoked duck eggs, Sichuan hot and spicy beef) and otherworldly puddings (ice cream with durian fruit, or glutinous rice and banana).

Ellen Leung
Founder of wholefood store Naturo+, Wan Chai

What's new in old Wan Chai? Our corner of Wan Chai is developing a personality of its own. There are galleries, tiny boutiques, great little bars, restaurants and, of course, our store and café. There's more on the way. The developers are trying to turn it into an arty area. **How come you ended up here?** I started Naturo+ (opposite) because I got tired of working for a big food group and I wanted to help peasants in China improve their income. We find trusted suppliers and connect them with the consumer. **What's inside the deli counter?** We've got Tibetan yak's cheese, wild honey collected from tree trunks in Yunan, rice from the Yixiang highlands, and Tongan coffee and spices. The quality is superb. We've even got some organic veg from Yuen Long in Hong Kong. **And on the café menu?** Come over for a wine or coffee tasting, or drop in for our special cheesecake, made from yak's milk. It's fantastic.

🍴 YÈ SHANGHAI 夜上海
Shanghainese $$

☎ 2918 9833; Shop 332, Level 3, Pacific Place, 88 Queensway, Admiralty; ⏱ 11.30am-3pm & 6-11.30pm; Ⓜ Admiralty 🔊

This is street hawker–style Shanghainese cuisine but with a few tweaks. The cold drunken pigeon is a Shao Xing wine-soaked winner and the steamed dumplings are perfectly plump, but sometimes this restaurant goes for clatter over substance. There's live music from 9pm to 11pm Thursday to Saturday.

🍴 YIN YANG 鴛鴦飯店
Cantonese $$$

☎ 2866 0868; 18 Ship St, Wan Chai; ⏱ noon-2.30pm & 7-10.30pm Mon-Sat; Ⓜ Wan Chai

Inspiration from the chef's Hakka roots, freshly made sauces, home-grown organic veg and old-style cooking techniques (including an old clay oven) combine to create some wonderfully flavoursome home-style cooking here, from the exotic (steamed sea urchin custard) to the everyday (lemon chicken). Book ahead.

🍸 DRINK

Wan Chai used to be all about avoiding the awful hostess bars along Lockhart Rd, while heading for the busy bar, club and live music action at the western ends of Jaffe and Lockhart Rds. This is the part of town that kicks on latest, but several worthwhile alternatives await south of the tram tracks in the resurgent little areas between Monmouth Place and St Francis St near Admiralty and around Ship St in Wan Chai.

🍸 1/5
Bar, Club

☎ 2520 2515; 1st fl, Starcrest Bldg, 9 Star St, Wan Chai; ⏱ 6pm-3am Mon-Thu, 6pm-4am Fri, 9pm-5am Sat, happy hr 6-9pm Mon-Fri; Ⓜ Admiralty

Pronounced 'one-fifth', this lounge bar-club has a broad bar backed by a two-storey drinks selection from which bar staff concoct some of Hong Kong's best cocktails. Thursday is salsa night.

🍸 CHAMPAGNE BAR
Bar, Live Music

☎ 2588 1234 ext 7321; Ground fl, Grand Hyatt Hong Kong, 1 Harbour Rd, Wan Chai; ⏱ 5pm-1am; Ⓜ Wan Chai

Take your fizz in the sumptuous surrounds of the Grand Hyatt's Champagne Bar, kitted out in art-deco furnishings realistic enough to evoke the Paris of the 1920s. Live blues or jazz rings through the bar most evenings, and the circular main bar is always busy.

☷ CHINATOWN 唐人街 *Bar*
☎ 2861 3588; 78-82 Jaffe Rd, Wan Chai; ☷ noon-2.30am, happy hr noon-6pm; Ⓜ Wan Chai
The soft lighting and large red lanterns combine to make this one of the more relaxed Wan Chai watering holes. The service from cheongsam-wearing waitresses is swift and friendly.

☷ DELANEY'S *Bar*
☎ 2804 2880; Ground & 1st fl, One Capital Place, 18 Luard Rd, Wan Chai; ☷ noon-3am, happy hr noon-9pm; Ⓜ Wan Chai
At this immensely popular Irish watering hole you can choose between the ground-floor pub, or the sports bar and restaurant on the 1st floor. There's also a branch in Tsim Sha Tsui.

☷ DEVIL'S ADVOCATE *Bar*
☎ 2865 7271; 48-50 Lockhart Rd, Wan Chai; ☷ noon-late Mon-Sat, 1pm-late Sun, happy hr noon-9pm daily, midnight-1am Fri & Sat; Ⓜ Wan Chai
This pleasant pub is as relaxed as they come. The bar spills out on to the pavement, and the staff are charming.

☷ MAYA *Bar*
☎ 2866 6200; 68-70 Lockhart Rd, Wan Chai; ☷ 11am-2am Sun-Thu, 11am-3am Fri & Sat, happy hr noon-9pm; Ⓜ Wan Chai

This lovely new bar has a name that apparently means 'illusion' in Sanskrit. It's a design-minded oasis in Wan Chai. We love the bold black-and-white patterns on the wall, the bright-red bar and, of course, the (almost) never-ending happy/relaxing/two-for-one hour(s).

☷ MES AMIS
Bar, Wine Bar
☎ 2527 6680; 83 Lockhart Rd, Wan Chai; ☷ noon-2.30am Sun-Tue & Thu, 5am Wed, noon-6am Fri & Sat, happy hr 4-9pm Mon-Thu, noon-9pm Sat & Sun; Ⓜ Wan Chai
This easygoing bar may be in the lap – so to speak – of girly club land but it's poles (again, as it were) apart. It has a good range of wine and a Mediterranean-style snack list. There's a DJ from 11pm on Wednesday, Friday and Saturday nights.

AMAH HOLIDAY
Explore central Hong Kong on a Sunday and you may notice a lot more people out and about, many of them young women gathered in groups, sitting, chatting, cooking and singing. These are Hong Kong's maids, the majority of them from the Philippines and Indonesia, grabbing what free space they can in parks and on pavements and enjoying their only day off.

🍺 PAWN *Pub*

☎ 2866 3444; 62 Johnston Rd, Wan Chai; ⏰ 11am-late; Ⓜ Wan Chai ♿

Downstairs from the Pawn's gastro-pub, the beaten-up sofas with space to sprawl make the ideal location to sample a great selection of lagers, bitters and wine at this excellent Wan Chai newcomer.

⭐ PLAY

⭐ AGNÈS B CINEMA *Cinema*

☎ 2582 0200; www.hkac.org.hk; Upper basement, Hong Kong Arts Centre, 2 Harbour Rd, Wan Chai; 🚌 18 Ⓜ Wan Chai

Despite its branded name, this very uncommercial cinema is *the* place for classics, revivals, alternative screenings and travelling film festivals.

⭐ CINE-ART HOUSE 影藝 *Cinema*

☎ 2827 4820; www.cityline.com.hk/eng/venues/cine_art.jsp; Ground fl, Sun Hung Kai Centre, 30 Harbour Rd, Wan Chai; tickets $65; 🚌 18 Ⓜ Wan Chai

This alternative cinema specialises in English-language films, but it's become a real hit-or-miss affair these days.

⭐ DUSK TILL DAWN *Live Music*

☎ 2528 4689; 76-84 Jaffe Rd, Wan Chai; ⏰ noon-7am Mon-Fri, 3pm-7am Sat & Sun, happy hr 5-9pm; Ⓜ Wan Chai

Live music from 10.30pm, with an emphasis on beats and vibes that will get your booty shaking. The dance floor can be packed, but the atmosphere is more friendly than sleazy. The food sticks to easy fillers such as meat pies and burgers.

⭐ HONG KONG ACADEMY FOR PERFORMING ARTS 香港演藝學院 *Theatre, Music*

☎ 2584 8500, bookings 3128 8288; www.hkapa.edu; 1 Gloucester Rd, Wan Chai; performances $80-750; Ⓜ Wan Chai ♿

Stages local and overseas performances of dance, drama and music. The building (1985), with its strik-

The local live music scene is rockin' at Wanch

WORTH THE TRIP

Just south of Wan Chai and accessible by tram from Hennessy Rd is the famous **Happy Valley Racecourse** (☎ 2895 1523, 2966 8111; http://racecourses.hkjc.com; 2 Sports Rd, Happy Valley; admission $10; ☷ from 7pm Wed Sep–early Jul; ☐ 75, 90, 97), a hugely atmospheric venue that buzzes on race nights when tens of thousands of punters come to wager millions of dollars. If the races aren't on, or your visit is during the day, there's also the esoteric but complete **Hong Kong Racing Museum** (☎ 2966 8065; www.hkjc .com; 2nd fl, Happy Valley Stand, Wong Nai Chung Rd; admission free; ☷ 10am-5pm Tue-Sun & most public holidays). If a day race meeting is being held, it's open from 10am to 12.30pm.

ing triangular atrium and exterior Meccano-like frame, was designed by local architect Simon Kwan.

⭐ HONG KONG ARTS CENTRE
香港藝術中心 *Theatre*
☎ 2582 0200; www.hkac.org.hk; 2 Harbour Rd, Wan Chai; performances $80-400; ☐ 18 Ⓜ Wan Chai
This independent contemporary arts centre showcases home-grown talent and its Shouson Theatre hosts drama (often in English). The centre also publishes a monthly listings magazine called *Artslink*. It's home to Pao Galleries (p80) and Agnès B Cinema (opposite).

⭐ JOE BANANA'S *Club*
☎ 2529 1811; Ground fl, Shiu Lam Bldg, 23 Luard Rd, Wan Chai; ☷ noon-5am Mon-Thu, noon-6am Fri, 4pm-6am Sat, 4pm-5am Sun, happy hr 6-10pm; Ⓜ Wan Chai

JB's, in Wan Chai forever (or at least since we were bopping and grooving), has dropped its long-standing wet T-shirt/boxers aesthetic and has opted for more of a bamboo-bar feel. The dancing is good and always makes for a fun night out.

⭐ WANCH
Live Music
☎ 2861 1621; 54 Jaffe Rd, Wan Chai; ☷ 11am-3am Mon-Fri, 2pm-3am Sat & Sun, happy hr 11am-10pm Mon-Fri, 2-10pm Sat & Sun; Ⓜ Wan Chai
The Wanch has live music (mostly rock and folk) happening nightly from 9pm or 10pm, with the oc-casional solo guitarist thrown in to the mix. Jam night is Wednes-day at 9pm. If you're not here for the music, well, the Wanch also has a reputation for being a seri-ous pulling place.

>HONG KONG ISLAND: CAUSEWAY BAY

Shopping is not the only reason to come to Causeway Bay, but it is the main one. Shoppers come for the massive Japanese department stores and the clusters of smaller outlets selling eclectic fashion in the neighbourhood's streets and mini-malls. Victoria Park at the eastern edge of the area is an ideal spot for some recreation, including a dip in the large outdoor pool or just for some respite from teeming crowds. The historic significance of the area to Hong Kong is, sadly, hardly visible today except in a few street names. Called Tung Lo Wan (Copper Gong Bay) in Cantonese, Causeway Bay was the site of a British settlement in the 1840s. It was also once an area of *godowns* (a Hong Kong business or pidgin English word for warehouses), and a well-protected harbour for fisherfolk and boatpeople. The new Causeway Bay, one of Hong Kong's top shopping areas, was built up from swampland and sand from the bottom of the harbour. Jardine Matheson, one of Hong Kong's largest *hongs* (major trading houses or companies), set up shop here, which explains why many of the streets in the district bear its name: Jardine's Bazaar, Jardine's Crescent and Yee Wo St (Cantonese for 'Jardine Matheson').

CAUSEWAY BAY

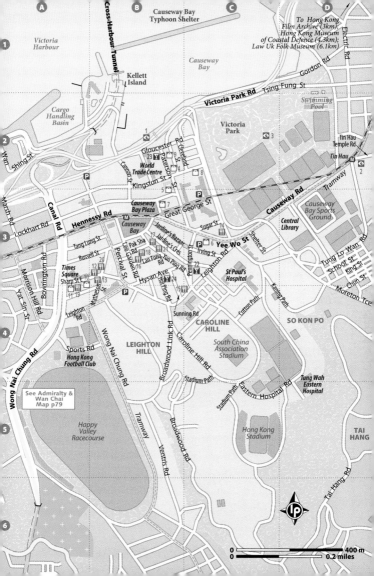

NEIGHBOURHOODS

HONG KONG ISLAND: CAUSEWAY BAY

👁 SEE

📷 NOONDAY GUN 午炮

221 Gloucester Rd, Causeway Bay; admission free; ⏱ subway access 7am-midnight; Ⓜ Causeway Bay (exit D1)

One of the few remnants of Causeway Bay's colonial past is this 3lb quick-firing cannon built by Hotchkiss of Portsmouth in 1901. It is fired daily at noon by a uniformed Jardine employee. Noel Coward made the gun famous with his satirical song 'Mad Dogs and Englishmen' (1924) about colonists who braved the heat of midday while local people stayed indoors: 'In Hong Kong/they strike a gong/and fire off a noonday gun/to reprimand each inmate/

who's in late.' The gun stands opposite the Excelsior Hong Kong hotel and is accessible via a tunnel under the road from the World Trade Centre basement, through a door marked 'Car Park Shroff, Marina Club & Noon Gun'.

📷 TIN HAU TEMPLE 天后廟

☎ 2721 2326; 10 Tin Hau Temple Rd, Causeway Bay; admission free; ⏱ 7am-6pm; Ⓜ Tin Hau (exit B) 🚻

Southeast of Victoria Park, Hong Kong Island's most famous Tin Hau temple is small; before reclamation in the last century this temple, dedicated to the patroness of seafarers, stood on the waterfront. It has been a place of worship for three centuries, though the current structure is only about 200 years old.

📷 VICTORIA PARK 維多利亞公園

☎ 2570 6186; www.lcsd.gov .hk/parks/vp/en/index.php; Causeway Rd, Causeway Bay; admission free; ⏱ 24hr; Ⓜ Causeway Bay (exit E), Tin Hau (exit A2) 🚻

At 17 hectares, Victoria Park is one of the biggest patches of public greenery in urban Hong Kong, and a popular city escape. The best time to take take a stroll around is during weekday mornings when it becomes a forest of people practising the slow-motion martial

SHOCK OF THE NEW

When Hong Kong's electric trams first started running more than a century ago, they caused a sensation. Stops were packed with people, but not many of them actually wanted to go anywhere; a great number just jumped on, walked through having a gawp and treading on toes, then got off again, not quite ready to ride. The trams were also delayed by hawkers who took advantage of the tramway by dragging their heavy carts along the well-made tracks. In 1911 a law was passed banning carts with the same wheel gauge as the trams. The law is still in effect today.

Causeway Bay's colonial past is still very much in daily action with the Noonday Gun

art of t'ai chi. The park becomes a vibrant flower market a few days before the Chinese New Year.

🛍 SHOP

Causeway Bay is a crush of department stores and smaller outlets selling eclectic fashion. Jardine's Bazaar has low-cost garments, and there are several sample shops for cheap jeans on Lee Garden Rd. There's a cluster of cool brands and independent clothing boutiques on the streets between Cleveland St and Victoria Park. The shops in the area open till late – 10pm.

🛍 CAMPER
Clothing & Accessories
☎ 2882 9310; 2 Kingston St, Causeway Bay; ⏰ noon-10pm; Ⓜ Causeway Bay
Camper, emblazoned with thought-provoking slogans and aphorisms out the front, is one of the most popular outlets in Hong Kong for locally designed fashion.

🛍 DADA CABARET VOLTAIRE
Clothing & Accessories
☎ 2890 1708; Shop F-13A, 1st fl, Fashion Island, 19 Great George St, Causeway Bay; ⏰ noon-10pm; Ⓜ Causeway Bay
Sells ragged rainbow colours that are also sported by the staff. This is just one of many fine shops in the

Fashion Island mini-mall complex. In the same mall see also the store called F.C.K. (Fashion Community Kitterick).

🎫 DELAY NO MALL
Department Store

☎ 2577 6988; 68 Yee Wo St, Causeway Bay; 🕐 noon-10pm; Ⓜ Causeway Bay

As much of an experience as a clothes shop, this supercool multifloor shop from the G.O.D. homewares chain is all about being on top of the latest trends, including retail ones. This magpie retail concept has a tattoo parlour, sleep pod installation and a bar-café (a branch of the slick FINDS bar-restaurant from Lan Kwai Fong; see p62). There's fashion, jewellery, homewares and beauty products from a well-selected group of hip brands.

🎫 ISLAND BEVERLEY
金百利商場
Clothing & Accessories

1 Great George St, Causeway Bay; Ⓜ Causeway Bay

Crammed into buildings, up escalators and in back lanes are Hong Kong's malls of micro-shops selling designer threads, a kaleidoscope of kooky accessories and an Imelda Marcos of funky footwear. Island Beverley is where Hong Kong's youngest mall trawlers shop for clothes and trinkets.

BAMBOO VS STEEL (& PLASTIC & WOOL…)

The bamboo scaffolding used to build even the tallest skyscrapers and lashed in place with plastic ties might look alarmingly low tech, but it works. Bamboo is lighter, cheaper and more flexible than bolted steel tubing and copes brilliantly with tensile stress, as you'll see if you watch builders scuttle around in their thin-soled slippers, barely causing a ripple. Product and industrial designers are now waking up to the potential of this green material, used in products as diverse as laptop casings, bicycle frames and even its softened fibres for clothing.

🎫 LCX
Clothing & Accessories

☎ 2890 5200; 9 Kingston St, Fashion Walk, Causeway Bay; 🕐 noon-10pm Mon-Fri, noon-10.30pm Sat & Sun; Ⓜ Causeway Bay

This high-end fashion outlet is a good example of the new stores sending Causeway Bay upmarket. Inside the stylishly lit plate glass you'll find clothes from top urban labels, including Marc Jacobs, Calvin Klein, Paul & Joe and Sonia Rykiel, plus upmarket beauty lines.

🎫 RUBY LI 李麗珊
Clothing & Accessories

☎ 2882 9303; 55 Paterson St, Causeway Bay; 🕐 noon-10pm Mon-Fri, noon-10.30pm Sat & Sun; Ⓜ Causeway Bay

A young up-and-coming Hong Kong designer, Li's look is modern with retro 1960s and '70s references and combines some sharp tailoring with flowing lines.

🗄 SPY
Clothing & Accessories
☎ 2893 7799; www.spyhenrylau.com; Shop C, ground fl, 11 Sharp St East, Causeway Bay; 🕙 1-11pm; Ⓜ Causeway Bay
Tame yet trendy everyday wear such as pants and short-sleeve shirts from designer Henry Lau.

🗄 WALTER MA 馬偉明
Clothing & Accessories
☎ 2838 7655; Ground fl, 33 Sharp St East; 🕙 noon-10pm Mon-Fri, noon-10.30pm Sat & Sun; Ⓜ Causeway Bay
Sophisticated but comfortable womenswear ranging from smart-casual office wear to more glamorous evening attire from the daddy of Hong Kong's home-grown fashion industry.

🍴 EAT

🍴 ARIRANG 阿里朗
Korean　　　　　　　$$
☎ 2506 3298; Shop 1105, 11th fl, Food Forum, Times Sq, 1 Matheson St, Causeway Bay; 🕙 noon-3pm & 6-11pm; Ⓜ Causeway Bay
A branch of the upmarket restaurant chain, with usual barbecues

along with excellent hotpot dishes. It's great for a bargain set lunch.

🍴 GO SUSHI 元綠壽司
Japanese　　　　　　$
☎ 2803 5909; 3 Matheson St, Causeway Bay; 🕙 11.30am-4am; Ⓜ Causeway Bay
Hong Kong's most exotic fast-food chain. The sushi tears around on a conveyor belt and is reasonably fresh. The only drawback is the potentially long wait for seats, especially during the manic lunch hour (1pm to 2pm). It's a great place for a late snack, though.

🍴 KUNG TAK LAM 功德林
Vegetarian, Chinese　　　$$
☎ 2881 9966; Ground fl, Lok Sing Centre, 31 Yee Wo St, Causeway Bay; 🕙 11am-11pm; Ⓜ Causeway Bay; Ⓥ
This long-established place, which serves Shanghai-style meatless dishes, has a more modern feel than most vegetarian eateries in Hong Kong. All vegies served are 100% organic and dishes are MSG free.

🍴 LE PAIN GRILLÉ
Café　　　　　　　$$$
☎ 2577 2718; Shop 1, ground fl, 111 Leighton Rd, Causeway Bay; 🕙 noon-10.30pm Sun-Thu, noon-11pm Fri & Sat; Ⓜ Causeway Bay
Ideal for a light lunch and afternoon tea, this calm little spot

NEIGHBOURHOODS

HONG KONG ISLAND: CAUSEWAY BAY

with dark wood tables and tiled floors makes for an ideal pre- or post-shopping pit stop. The menu is stuffed with French classics, including onion soup, snails, *confit de canard* (preserved duck) and slow-cooked spring chicken.

If you want to set your palate alight, try this friendly, long-established eatery's sliced pork in chilli sauce, accompanied by *dan dan min* (noodles in a spicy peanut broth). Also recommended are the deep-fried beans and sizzling prawns.

🍴 RED PEPPER 南北樓
Sichuanese $$
☎ 2577 3811; 7 Lan Fong Rd, Causeway Bay; 🕙 11.30am-midnight;
Ⓜ Causeway Bay

🍴 SUSHI HIRO 壽司廣
Japanese $$$
☎ 2882 8752; 10th fl, Henry House, 42 Yun Ping Rd, Causeway Bay; 🕙 noon-11pm, to 10.30pm Sun; Ⓜ Causeway Bay

WORTH THE TRIP
A handful of top-class museums make a trip along the island's northern coast more worthwhile.

The history of Hong Kong's once booming and hard-boiled film industry is interesting and the **Hong Kong Film Archive** (☎ 2739 2139; www.filmarchive.gov.hk; 50 Lei King Rd, Sai Wan Ho; admission free; 🕙 10am-8pm, resource centre 10am-7pm Mon-Wed & Fri, 10am-5pm Sat, 1-5pm Sun; Ⓜ Sai Wan Ho, exit A) is the place to hear (and watch) it. The archive houses some 5600 films, runs a rich calendar of local and foreign movie screenings in its 127-seat **cinema** (☎ 2734 9009; tickets $30-50; 🕙 box office noon-8pm Mon-Wed & Fri-Sun), and exhibits wonderful posters and other fine film paraphernalia. Check the website for screenings and times.

The history of Hong Kong's coastal defences and battles is well presented at **Hong Kong Museum of Coastal Defence** (☎ 2569 1500; www.lcsd.gov.hk/ce/museum/coastal; 175 Tung Hei Rd, Shau Kei Wan; adult/child $10/5, free Wed; 🕙 10am-5pm Fri-Wed; 🚌 84, 85 Ⓜ Shau Kei Wan, exit B2, then 15min walk north along Tung Hei Rd) in restored Lei Yue Mun Fort (1887), which took quite a beating during WWII. Exhibits in the old redoubt cover the Ming and Qing dynasties, the colonial years, the Japanese invasion and the return of Hong Kong to Chinese sovereignty. There's a historical trail through casements, tunnels and observation posts almost down to the coast.

The small **Law Uk Folk Museum** (☎ 2896 7006; http://hk.history.museum; 14 Kut Shing St, Chai Wan; admission free; 🕙 10am-1pm & 2-6pm Mon-Wed, Fri & Sat, 1-6pm Sun; Ⓜ Chai Wan, exit B) offers a simple but charming presentation of traditional rural life from two restored Hakka village houses that have been declared a historical monument. The quiet courtyard and surrounding bamboo groves are peaceful and evocative.

One of several excellent, if low-key, Japanese places hidden in the area's high-rise offices, Sushi Hiro offers seasonal choices of fish that change on a weekly basis. Set lunch starts from $130 per head (nine pieces) and set dinner $320 (12 pieces). Very reasonable value given the quality.

🍴 TAI PING KOON
太平館餐廳
International, Chinese $$$
☎ 2576 9161; 6 Pak Sha Rd, Causeway Bay; 🕑 11am-midnight; Ⓜ Causeway Bay
This place has been around since 1860 and offers an incredible mix of Western and Chinese flavours – what Hong Kong people called 'soy sauce restaurants' in pre-fusion days. Try the borscht and the smoked pomfret or some roast pigeon, all specialities of the house.

🍴 W'S ENTRECÔTE
French, Steakhouse $$
☎ 2506 0133; www.wsentrecote.com; 6th fl, Express by Holiday Inn, 33 Sharp St East, Causeway Bay; 🕑 noon-3pm & 6-10.30pm; Ⓜ Causeway Bay
W's serves steak almost exclusively in a number of shapes and sizes but with a Gallic twist. Included in the price is a salad and as many *frites* (chips) as you can squeeze onto your plate. Entrées are in the 'foie gras and snails' category.

Try some Sichaunese specialities at Red Pepper

🍴 WASABISABI
Japanese $$$
☎ 2506 0009; Shop 1301, 13th fl, Food Forum, Times Sq, 1 Matheson St, Causeway Bay; 🕑 noon-3pm daily, 6pm-midnight Sun-Thu, 6pm-2am Fri & Sat; Ⓜ Causeway Bay
Excellent Japanese cuisine, impeccable service and an over-the-top interior. From cable vines through to lipstick reds and into the sweeping sushi bar of palm leaves and ostrich feathers, this is eclectic magnificence. The bar turns into a club at night.

NEIGHBOURHOODS

HONG KONG ISLAND: CAUSEWAY BAY

The East End Brewery stocks local Hong Kong beers, alongside a large range of imported microbrews and ales

🍴 XINJISHI 新吉士
Shanghainese $$

☎ 2890 1122; Shop 201-203, 2nd fl, Lee Gardens Two, 28 Yun Ping Rd; 🕑 noon-3pm & 6-11pm; Ⓜ Causeway Bay

A branch of a successful mainland-based chain, serving traditional Shanghainese (the cooks are imported) in a modern, very stylish setting. Try one of the clay-pot dishes, such as braised pork meatballs with vegetables ($70).

🍸 DRINK

Unlike Wan Chai, Central or Soho, Causeway Bay is hardly the life and soul. The bars tend to be sparsely frequented here (unless the Rubgy Sevens crowds are in town). Look out for developments at boutique hotel JIA, which will host a cool little bar following a recent fit-out.

🍸 BRECHT'S CIRCLE *Bar*

☎ 2577 9636, 2576 4785; www .brechts.net; Ground fl, Rita House, 123 Leighton Rd, Causeway Bay; 🕑 4pm-2am Sun-Thu, 4pm-4am Fri & Sat, happy hr 4-8pm; Ⓜ Causeway Bay

This is a very small and fairly unusual clublike bar. It's a place given more to intimate, cerebral conversation than serious raging. A good place to seek out if you don't fancy the peanut-shell cracking bustle of the East End Brewery.

☒ DICKENS BAR *Pub*

☎ 2837 6782; Basement, Excelsior Hong Kong, 281 Gloucester Rd, Causeway Bay; ◷ 11am-1am Sun-Thu, 11am-2am Fri & Sat, happy hr 5-8pm; Ⓜ Causeway Bay

It's ill-lit, the decor is heavy and it's in a basement. The perfect ingredients for that old-fashioned British-pub atmosphere. This long-standing institution remains a popular spot for expats and Hong Kong Chinese alike. There's a very popular curry buffet lunch and lots of big-screen sports.

☒ INN SIDE OUT & EAST END BREWERY *Pub*

☎ 2895 2900; Ground fl, Sunning Plaza, 10 Hysan Ave, Causeway Bay; ◷ 11am-1am Sun-Thu, 11am-1.30am Fri & Sat, happy hr 2.30-8.30pm; Ⓜ Causeway Bay

These two pubs flank a central covered terrace where you can while away the hours on a warm evening, sipping microbrewed beers and enjoying free peanuts, happily throwing your shells on the ground.

>HONG KONG ISLAND: ISLAND SOUTH

In complete contrast to the frantic northern shore of Hong Kong Island, its southern extent affords space and relaxation. From Big Wave Bay and Shek O in the east to Aberdeen and Ap Lei Chau in the west, the area is full of attractions and things to do. This is Hong Kong Island's backyard playground – from the good beaches of Repulse Bay, Deep Water Bay and Shek O, to shoppers' paradise Stanley Market and the excellent Ocean Park amusement park near Aberdeen, which packs in enough entertainment for a whole day. The island also has its own little bit of wilderness threaded through by one of Hong Kong's most enjoyable long-range walks, the 78km Wilson Trail, which starts just north of Stanley. In general, the best way to get around this part of Hong Kong Island is by the excellent and extensive bus service. Ride up front on the upper deck and you get a white-knuckle ride thrown in free as the bus navigates narrow, twisting mountain roads. If time is short, taxis are not too cripplingly expensive.

ISLAND SOUTH

🅖 SEE
Hong Kong Maritime
    Museum 1 F4
Ocean Park 2 C2
Repulse Bay 3 E2

🅐 SHOP
Stanley Market 4 F4

🍴 EAT
Lucy's 5 F4
Shu Zai 6 F4
Top Deck at the Jumbo ... 7 C2
Verandah 8 E2

NEIGHBOURHOODS

HONG KONG ISLAND: ISLAND SOUTH

◉ SEE

◉ HONG KONG MARITIME MUSEUM
香港海事博物館

☎ 2813 2322; www.hkmaritime museum.org; Ground fl, Murray House, Stanley Plaza, Stanley; adult/child $20/10; ☽ 10am-6pm Tue-Fri & Sun, 10am-7pm Sat; ☒ 6, 6A, 6X, 260; ⛑

This small but worthwhile museum in Stanley's Murray House (see boxed text, below) is well worth a look when you're in Stanley. Highlights include some wonderful mock-ups of Tang dynasty seagoing vessels, a nice collection of trade art (including sketches by celebrated 19th-century painter George Chinnery) and a fair amount of hands-on exhibits, including a simulator that allows you to sit on the bridge of a container ship and guide it (maybe) into Victoria Harbour.

◉ OCEAN PARK 香港海洋公園

☎ 2552 0291; www.oceanpark .com.hk; Ocean Park Rd, Aberdeen; adult/child $208/103; ☽ 10am-6pm; ☒ 6X, 73, 629 (Ocean Park Citybus), green minibus 6; ⛑

Don't miss Hong Kong's biggest home-grown theme park. It amuses and educates with roller coasters, giant pandas, the world's largest aquarium and an atoll reef. The two-part complex is linked by a scenic (slightly hair-raising) cable-car ride. The park entrance is on the lowland side southeast of Aberdeen and the main section is on the headlands, with terrific views of the South China Sea.

◉ REPULSE BAY 淺水灣

☒ 6, 6A, 6X or 260

Though it can get packed on weekends, and even during the week in summer, the long beach at Repulse Bay is a good place if you like people-watching. At its southeastern end is an unusual

A CHINESE PUZZLE

When the Hong Kong government pulled down Hong Kong's oldest colonial building in 1982 to make room for the new Bank of China, it promised to rebuild **Murray House** (above) elsewhere at a later date. The time finally came in the mid-1990s and the place chosen was Stanley – but the pieces had been so badly numbered and catalogued that it took workers 3½ years to put this colossal puzzle back together again on a wonderful waterfront location in Stanley village. Unfortunately, when they'd finished, they didn't know what to do with six extra columns. You'll see them standing idly to the left along the waterfront promenade.

The colourful stalls at Stanley Market can cause sensory overload

shrine to Kwun Yam, the deity of Mercy. The surrounding area has an amazing assembly of mosaics, gods and figures – goldfish, rams, statues of Tin Hau and other southern Chinese icons. In front of the shrine, to the left as you face the sea, is Longevity Bridge; crossing it is supposed to add three days to your life. See also boxed text, p105.

🛍 SHOP

🛍 STANLEY MARKET 赤柱市集
Market

Stanley Village Rd, Stanley; 🕐 **9am-6pm;** 🚌 **6, 6A, 6X, 260**
No big bargains nor big stings, just reasonably priced casual clothes (plenty of large sizes), linens, hats, bric-a-brac, toys and formulaic art,

NEIGHBOURHOODS

HONG KONG ISLAND: ISLAND SOUTH

all in a nicely confusing maze of alleys running down to Stanley Bay. It's best to go during the week if possible.

EAT

LUCY'S *International* $$$

☎ 2813 9055; 64 Stanley Main St, Stanley; ⏱ noon-3pm & 7-10pm Mon-Fri, noon-4pm & 6.30-9.30pm Sat & Sun; 🚌 6, 6A, 6X, 260

This very relaxed place doesn't overwhelm with choice but with quality. The menu changes frequently depending on the fresh produce to hand and the inspiration to use it, but the offerings tend towards honest fusion rather than flimflammery. There's a good selection of wines by the glass.

SHU ZHAI 書齋

Chinese $$

☎ 2813 0123; 80 Stanley Main St, Stanley; ⏱ noon-10pm; 🚌 6, 6A, 6X or 260

Modelled to resemble a school in ancient China, this breezy new restaurant off Stanley's waterfront serves an assortment of Chinese dishes that are as nice to look at as to eat. Braised Mandarin fish with vermicelli in salty sauce ($148) is a must try.

Getting there is half the fun – sampan is the only way to go to the Jumbo Floating Restaurant

HOLE IN THE SOUL

The executives' playground of **Repulse Bay** (p102) is surrounded by swanky high-rise apartment blocks. Among them is a giant pink, blue and yellow wavy structure with a giant square hole in the middle called 'The Repulse Bay'. Apparently this design feature was added on the advice of a feng shui expert.

🍴 TOP DECK AT THE JUMBO
Chinese $$$

☎ 2552 3331; www.cafedecogroup .com; Jumbo Kingdom, Shum Wan Pier Dr, Wong Chuk Hang, Aberdeen; 🕐 11.30am-midnight Tue-Thu & Sun, 11.30am-1am Fri & Sat; 🚌 70, 73, 973

This new spin on a Hong Kong institution sits atop the Jumbo Kingdom, the larger of two floating restaurants moored in Aberdeen Harbour. But while the restaurant below offers lacklustre seafood and a 'Beijing's Imperial Palace meets Las Vegas casino' decor, the Top Deck promises grown-up food and delightful surrounds. The Sunday unlimited seafood and champagne buffet is a great splurge. There's free transport for diners from the pier on Aberdeen Promenade.

🍴 VERANDAH
International, Asian $$$

☎ 2292 2822; 1st fl, The Repulse Bay, 109 Repulse Bay Rd, Repulse Bay 🕐 breakfast 7-10am Mon-Sat, 7-10.30am Sun, brunch & lunch noon-3pm, afternoon tea 3-5.30pm, dinner 6.30-11pm; 🚌 6, 6A, 6X, 260

This place is housed in a replicated colonial structure in front of the wavy Repulse Bay condos (see boxed text, left), which is meant to recall the stunning Repulse Bay Hotel that was bulldozed in 1982. Wooden ceiling fans swooshing away, palms in their pots and a sea-facing outlook all lend a tropical feel. The Verandah is hushed and formal with heavy white tablecloths and demurely clinking cutlery. The brunch is famous (book well ahead), and the afternoon tea is the south side's best.

>KOWLOON: TSIM SHA TSUI & TSIM SHA TSUI EAST

Tsim Sha Tsui (Sharp Sandy Point; roughly pronounced chim-sa-choy) is a vibrant area and holds one big trump card: an unforgettable view of Hong Kong Island in all its riotous high-rise grandeur. This is also the bit of town to suck up some culture; the area is thick with museums, galleries and performance spaces. More than anything else Tsim Sha Tsui is about shopping. Countless clothing and shoe shops, camera and electronics stores, and hotels are somehow crammed into an area not much bigger than 1 sq km. But beware: Nathan Rd, the main tourist strip here, is one of the very few places where you'll find merchants poised to rip you off, especially when buying electronic goods or photographic equipment.

TSIM SHA TSUI & TSIM SHA TSUI EAST

◉ SEE
Chungking Mansions 1 C3
Former Marine Police
  Headquarters 2 C4
Hong Kong Museum
  of Art 3 C4
Hong Kong Museum
  of History................4 E1
Hong Kong Science
  Museum 5 E2
Hong Kong Space
  Museum 6 C4
KCR Clock Tower 7 C4
Kowloon Mosque
  & Islamic Centre......8 C2
Kowloon Park 9 C2
Peninsula Hotel
  Hong Kong............10 C3
Tsim Sha Tsui
  Promenade............11 C4

🏠 SHOP
Alan Chan Creations ... (see 10)
Beatniks 12 D2

Chinese Arts & Crafts ...13 B4
i.t. 14 D2
Lane Crawford............15 B4
Om International..........16 D3
Onesto Photo Company..17 D2
Opal Mine 18 C2
Page One 19 B3
Premier Jewellery 20 D3
Star Computer City......21 C4
Swindon Book Co. Ltd ..22 C3
Travelmax...................(see 15)
www.izzue.com............23 B3

🍴 EAT
Aqua 24 C3
Chang Won Korean
  Restaurant 25 D2
Dan Ryan's Chicago Grill...26 B3
Eastern Palace Chiu
  Chow Restaurant 27 B4
Fat Angelo's................28 D3
Felix...........................29 C3
Fook Lam Moon...........30 D2
Gaylord......................31 C3

Good Satay 32 E3
Hutong ....(see 24)
Merhaba.....................33 D1
Nadaman....................34 E3
Nobu..........................(see 40)
Sabatini......................35 E2
Wu Kong Shanghai
  Restaurant 36 C3
Yummy Vietnamese
  Restaurant 37 B2

🍸 DRINK
Bar ....(see 29)
Biergarten...................38 D3
Chillax.......................39 D3
Felix...........................(see 29)
Lobby Lounge.............40 D4
Sky Lounge.................41 D3

★ PLAY
Bahama Mama's...........42 D1
Cloudnine...................43 D3
Hari's.........................44 C3
Hong Kong Cultural
  Centre....................45 C4

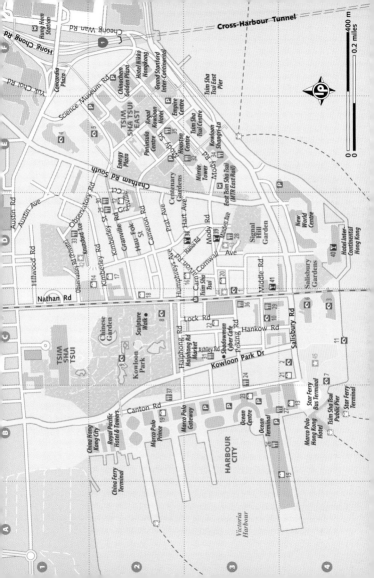

👁 SEE

👁 CHUNGKING MANSIONS 重慶大廈

☎ 36-44 Nathan Rd, Tsim Sha Tsui; admission free; Ⓜ Tsim Sha Tsui (exit D1)
Say 'budget accommodation' and 'Hong Kong' in one breath and everyone thinks of Chungking Mansions, a place like no other in the world. This huge, ramshackle high-rise dump in the heart of Tsim Sha Tsui caters to virtually all needs – from finding a bed and a curry lunch to changing your Burmese kyat and getting your hair cut – but you may be put off by the undercurrent of sleaze and the peculiar odour of cooking fat, incense and sewage. The building's infamy is fuelled by tales both tall and true of conflagrations, crimes and unclaimed bodies; everyone should come here once. The entrance to Chungking Mansions is via Chungking Arcade, a parade of shops that faces Nathan Rd. See also p17.

👁 FORMER MARINE POLICE HEADQUARTERS 前水警總部

Salisbury Rd, Tsim Sha Tsui; admission free; Ⓜ Tsim Sha Tsui (exit E) 🚢 Star Ferry (Tsim Sha Tsui)
Still a building site at the time of writing, this handsome declared monument with a boutique hotel and upscale shops should be

trading by this book's publication as an extensive and lengthy redevelopment of this prime site overlooking the harbour.

👁 HONG KONG MUSEUM OF ART 香港藝術博物館

☎ 2721 0116; http://hk.art.museum; 10 Salisbury Rd, Tsim Sha Tsui; adult/child $10/5, free Wed; ⏰ 10am-6pm Sun-Fri, 10am-8pm Sat; Ⓜ Tsim Sha Tsui (exit E) 🚢 Star Ferry (Tsim Sha Tsui)
This museum does a credible job of showing classical Chinese art, paintings and lithographs of old Hong Kong and (mostly) calligraphy in the Xubaizhi collection in a total of seven galleries spread over six floors. There are also exquisite ceramics and gold artefacts plus a few worthwhile international exhibitions.

👁 HONG KONG MUSEUM OF HISTORY 香港歷史博物館

☎ 2724 9042; http://hk.history .museum; 100 Chatham Rd South, Tsim Sha Tsui East; adult/child $10/5, free Wed; ⏰ 10am-6pm Mon & Wed-Sat, 10am-7pm Sun; Ⓜ Tsim Sha Tsui (exit A2) 🚌 5, 8
Hong Kong's best museum after the Hong Kong Heritage Museum (p138) focuses on the territory's archaeology, natural history, ethnography and local history. It's well worth a visit to understand how Hong Kong presents its

history to itself and the world (p21). Free guided tours of the museum are available in English at 10.30am and 2.30pm on Saturday and Sunday.

◉ HONG KONG SCIENCE MUSEUM 香港科學館

☎ 2732 3232; http://hk.science .museum; 2 Science Museum Rd, Tsim Sha Tsui East; adult/child $25/12.50, free Wed; 🕙 1-9pm Mon-Wed & Fri, 10am-9pm Sat & Sun; Ⓜ Tsim Sha Tsui (exit A2) 🚌 5, 5C, 8

The Hong Kong Science Museum is a multilevel complex with more than 500 displays on computers, energy, physics, robotics, telecommunications, health and various other subjects in 18 galleries. Although some of the exhibits are beginning to look a little dated, the numerous buttons to push and robot arms to operate – especially on the mammoth Energy Machine – will keep young (and some older) visitors entertained.

◉ HONG KONG SPACE MUSEUM 香港太空館

☎ 2721 0226; http://hk.space .museum; 10 Salisbury Rd, Tsim Sha Tsui; adult/child $10/5, free Wed; 🕙 1-9pm Mon & Wed-Fri, 10am-9pm Sat & Sun; Ⓜ Tsim Sha Tsui (exit E) 🚢 Star Ferry (Tsim Sha Tsui)

Just east of the Kowloon Cultural Centre, this golf ball–shaped building is a passable rainy day option, consisting of the Hall of Space Science on the ground floor and the Hall of Astronomy and Stanley Ho Space Theatre planetarium on the 1st floor. Exhibits include a lump of moon rock, rocket-ship models and NASA's 1962 *Mercury* space capsule, and you can experience a simulated moon walk. The space theatre screens 'sky shows' and Omnimax films (adult/child stalls $32/16, front stalls $24/12, first show 1.30pm Monday to Friday, 12.20pm Saturday, 11.10am Sunday) mostly in Cantonese, with translations by audiophone.

NEIGHBOURHOODS

KOWLOON: TSIM SHA TSUI & TSIM SHA TSUI EAST

◎ KCR CLOCK TOWER
尖沙咀前九廣鐵路鐘樓

Star Ferry Terminal, Salisbury Rd, Tsim Sha Tsui; Ⓜ **Tsim Sha Tsui (exit E)** 🚢 **Star Ferry (Tsim Sha Tsui)**

This 44m-high clock tower, built in 1915, is all that remains of the southern terminus of the Kowloon-Canton Railway (KCR), inaugurated in 1916 and torn down in 1978. The original colonial building was too small to handle the large volume of passenger traffic and operations moved to the modern station at Hung Hom.

◎ KOWLOON MOSQUE & ISLAMIC CENTRE 九龍清真寺

☎ **2724 0095; 105 Nathan Rd, Tsim Sha Tsui; admission free;** 🕒 **5am-10pm;** Ⓜ **Tsim Sha Tsui (exit A1)**

Hong Kong's largest mosque, completed in 1984, occupies the site of a previous mosque built in 1896 for Muslim Indian troops garrisoned in barracks at what is now known as Kowloon Park (right). The mosque has a handsome dome, minarets and a carved marble exterior. It is capable of accommodating 7000 worshippers. Muslims are welcome to attend services at the mosque but non-Muslims should ask permission to enter. If you do visit, remove your shoes before entering.

◎ KOWLOON PARK 九龍公園

☎ **2724 3344; www.lcsd.gov.hk/parks/ kp/en/index.php; 22 Austin Rd, Tsim Sha Tsui; admission free;** 🕒 **6am-midnight;** Ⓜ **Tsim Sha Tsui (exit A1), Jordan (exit C1)**

Built on the site of a barracks for Muslim Indian soldiers in the colonial army, Kowloon Park is an oasis of greenery and a refreshing escape from the hustle and bustle of Tsim Sha Tsui. Pathways and walls criss-cross the grass, birds hop around in cages, and towers and viewpoints dot the landscape. The Sculpture Walk features works by local and international sculptors. While it's not a must-visit, the modest Hong Kong Discovery Centre is worth a look if you're interested in Hong Kong's architectural heritage.

◎ PENINSULA HOTEL HONG KONG 香港半島酒店

☎ **2920 2888; www.peninsula.com; cnr Salisbury & Nathan Rds, Tsim Sha Tsui;** Ⓜ **Tsim Sha Tsui (exit E)**

More than a Hong Kong landmark, the Peninsula, in the thronelike building opposite the Hong Kong Space Museum, is one of the world's great hotels. Land reclamation has robbed the hotel of its top waterfront location, but the breathtaking lobby of the original building is well worth a visit. And it's by far the classiest place in town to take tea. See also p17.

Raymond Lo
Feng Shui Master

So. Feng shui. What's all that about then? Feng shui is an ancient study of the way the environment affects people's well-being. It recognises there are different kinds of energy, some negative, some positive. **How do you use this knowledge?** I apply its principles to help people live happily and prosperously. It helps decide where the boss should sit in an office building or how to arrange a home for health and wealth. I also help people pick auspicious wedding days. **What are Hong Kong's feng shui vibes like?** It has the best feng shui of anywhere I've visited. It forms the end of the massive Southern Dragon coming from China, creating a unique landscape that concentrates energy in the harbour. Feng shui practitioners describe this as 'the dragon turning its head to greet the ancestor'. **What's the best-placed spot to soak up all this good feng shui?** The Peninsula Hotel (opposite) and Statue Square (p46), in front of the HSBC building, are good. Repulse Bay (p102) is another very special spot; it's known as the Dragon's Den.

◐ TSIM SHA TSUI PROMENADE
尖沙咀海濱長廊

South of Salisbury Rd along Victoria Harbour, Tsim Sha Tsui; admission free; ⚓ Star Ferry (Tsim Sha Tsui), hydrofoil (Tsim Sha Tsui East Pier)

Stretching along what is arguably the most dramatic harbour in the world, this open-air walkway offers superb views of Hong Kong Island. Along the first part of the promenade the underwhelming Avenue of the Stars pays homage to the Hong Kong film industry and its stars, with handprints, sculptures and information boards. The promenade is a lovely place to stroll during the day, but it's best at night when the Symphony of Lights, a spectacular sound-and-light show involving more than 33 buildings (21 of them on the Hong Kong Island skyline), takes place from 8pm to 8.20pm daily. See also p11.

🛍 SHOP

🏠 ALAN CHAN CREATIONS
東西坊 *Gifts & Souvenirs*

☎ 2723 2722; www.alanchancreations.com; Shop 5A, Basement, Peninsula Hotel Hong Kong, cnr Salisbury & Nathan Rds, Tsim Sha Tsui; ⏰ 9.30am-7pm; Ⓜ Tsim Sha Tsui (exit E) ⚓ Star Ferry (Tsim Sha Tsui)

Alan Chan has designed everything – from airport logos to soy-sauce bottles – and now lends his name to stylish souvenirs, such as clothing and ceramic pieces. Some items he has a direct hand in, others he simply approves of. Cool, contemporary Chinese design that should inspire plenty of gift ideas.

🏠 BEATNIKS
Clothing & Accessories

☎ 2739 8494; Shop 1, Rise Commercial Bldg, Granville Circuit, Tsim Sha Tsui; ⏰ 11am-9pm; Ⓜ Tsim Sha Tsui ⚓ Star Ferry (Tsim Sha Tsui)

A selective stock ensures that a visit to this vintage clothing outlet isn't like the jumble-sale rummage you get with many secondhand outlets. The focus here is on street styles and left-field cool, rather than on high fashion or couture.

BUYER BEWARE

Hong Kong is a trustworthy place to shop, but it's worth bearing a couple of things in mind. Most shops are loath to give refunds but they can usually be persuaded to exchange purchases that can be resold; just make sure you get a receipt. When buying electronic goods, always beware of merchandise imported by an unauthorised agent, as this may void your warranty. A good marker of trustworthy merchants is the Quality Tourism Services logo (which should be displayed on the front door). If you experience problems, call the **Hong Kong Consumer Council** (☎ 2929 2222; www.consumer.org.hk).

◻ CHINESE ARTS & CRAFTS 中藝 Gifts & Souvenirs

☎ 2735 4061; www.crcretail.com; 1st fl, Star House, 3 Salisbury Rd, Tsim Sha Tsui; ◷ 10am-9.30pm; Ⓜ Tsim Sha Tsui 🚢 Star Ferry (Tsim Sha Tsui)

This Aladdin's department store of high-end gifts and souvenirs is probably the best place to buy quality bric-a-brac and other Chinese *chotchkies* (cheap, flashy trinkets).

◻ GRANVILLE RD FACTORY OUTLETS Clothing & Accessories

Granville Rd, Tsim Sha Tsui; Ⓜ Tsim Sha Tsui

If you have the time and inclination to rifle through racks and piles of factory seconds, the dozen or so factory outlets selling slightly premium mainstream casual and leisure brands along Granville Rd (Map p107, D2) should reward you with costs a fraction of store price. Hotspots include UNO OUN (No 29), Sample Moon (No 30) and the Baleno Outlet Store (No 24B).

◻ I.T Clothing & Accessories

☎ 2736 9152; Shop 1030, 1st fl, Miramar Shopping Centre, 1-23 Kimberley Rd, Tsim Sha Tsui; ◷ noon-10pm; Ⓜ Tsim Sha Tsui

This shop and the women's-only b+ab shop next door both sell stylish mainstream fashion fairly typical of the type that abounds in Hong Kong, although it's a notch up in quality and price from the likes of Bossini. There are i.t shops in all the major shopping areas.

◻ LANE CRAWFORD 連卡佛 Department Store

☎ 2118 3428; www.lanecrawford.com; Ground & 1st fl, Ocean Terminal, Harbour City, Salisbury Rd; ◷ 10am-9pm; Ⓜ Tsim Sha Tsui 🚢 Star Ferry (Tsim Sha Tsui)

Hong Kong's first (and most successful) Western-style department store is still a very upmarket place – rather like the British department store Harvey Nichols (which has opened across the harbour in The Landmark Mall).

Swindon Book Co. Ltd has tomes to suit all tastes at its Tsim Sha Tsui store

OM INTERNATIONAL
Jewellery

☎ 2366 3421; www.omperals.com; Ste A3, 1st fl, Friend's House, 6 Carnarvon Rd, Tsim Sha Tsui; 🕙 9.30am-6pm Mon-Sat; Ⓜ Tsim Sha Tsui

An excellent selection of saltwater and freshwater pearls awaits you here, with a lot more on offer than what you see. The staff is friendly, helpful and very honest.

ONESTO PHOTO COMPANY
忠誠 *Photographic Equipment*

☎ 2723 4668; Shop 18, block B, ground fl, Champagne Crt, 16 Kimberley Rd, Tsim Sha Tsui; 🕙 10.30am-8.30pm Mon-Sat, 11am-7pm Sun; Ⓜ Tsim Sha Tsui

This retail outlet, which stocks mostly film cameras, has price tags on its equipment (a rarity in Tsim Sha Tsui) but there's always a bit of latitude for bargaining.

OPAL MINE 澳之寶有限公司
Jewellery

☎ 2721 9933; www.opalnet.com; Shop G & H, ground fl, Burlington Arcade, 92-94 Nathan Rd, Tsim Sha Tsui; 🕙 9.30am-7pm; Ⓜ Tsim Sha Tsui

More of a museum than a shop, this place lives up to its name with a truly vast selection of Australian opals that makes for fascinating viewing and buying, should you be so tempted.

PAGE ONE *Books*
☎ 2730 6080; www.pageonegroup.com; Shop 3202, 3rd fl, Gateway Arcade, Harbour City, Canton Rd, Tsim Sha Tsui; 🕑 10.30am-10pm Mon-Thu, 10.30am-10.30pm Fri-Sun; Ⓜ Tsim Sha Tsui 🚢 Star Ferry (Tsim Sha Tsui)

A chain, yes, but a good one. Page One has Hong Kong's best selection of art and design magazines and books, and it's also strong on photography, literature, film and children's books.

PREMIER JEWELLERY
愛寶珠寶 *Jewellery*
☎ 2368 0003; Shop G14-15, ground fl, Holiday Inn Golden Mile Shopping Mall, 50 Nathan Rd, Tsim Sha Tsui; 🕑 10am-7.30pm Mon-Sat, 10.30am-4pm Sun; Ⓜ Tsim Sha Tsui

This family business is directed by a qualified gemologist and is a firm favourite. If you're looking for something in particular, give them a day's notice to have a selection ready for you. They can also help you design your own piece.

STAR COMPUTER CITY
星光電腦城 *Computers*
☎ 2736 2608; 2nd fl, Star House, 3 Salisbury Rd, Tsim Sha Tsui; 🕑 10am or 10.30am-7.30pm or 8pm; Ⓜ Tsim Sha Tsui 🚢 Star Ferry (Tsim Sha Tsui)

This is the largest complex of computer outlets in Tsim Sha Tsui, with two dozen shops selling laptops, personal organisers and Apple computers. It's not as cheap as the computer malls in Mongkok or New Kowloon, but it is better set up for international buyers.

SWINDON BOOK CO. LTD
辰衝 *Books*
☎ 2366 8001; www.swindonbooks.com; 13-15 Lock Rd, Tsim Sha Tsui; 🕑 9am-6.30pm Mon-Thu, 9am-7.30pm Fri & Sat, 12.30-6.30pm Sun; Ⓜ Tsim Sha Tsui

This is one of the best 'real' (as opposed to 'supermarket') bookshops. Its sister store is Central's Hong Kong Book Centre (p49).

TRAVELMAX *Outdoor Gear*
☎ 3188 4271; Shop 270-273, 2nd fl, Ocean Terminal, Harbour City, Salisbury Rd; 🚢 Star Ferry (Tsim Sha Tsui)

Travelmax sells both lightweight and cold-weather outdoor gear;

SHIPPING NEWS

Goods can be mailed home by post, and some shops will package and post the goods for you. It's a good idea to find out whether you will have to clear the goods through customs at the other end. If the goods are fragile, it's sensible to buy 'all risks' insurance. Smaller items can be shipped from the post office. **United Parcel Service** (UPS; ☎ 2735 3535) also offers services from Hong Kong to some 200 destinations. **DHL Express** (☎ 2400 3388), with outlets in many MTR stations, is another option.

kids' sizes are available. There's a good range of Eagle Creek travel products here, too.

🛒 WWW.IZZUE.COM
Clothing & Accessories

☎ 2992 0631; www.izzue.com; Shop 2225, 2nd fl, Gateway Arcade, Harbour City, Canton Rd, Tsim Sha Tsui; 🕙 11am-9pm; Ⓜ Tsim Sha Tsui 🚢 Star Ferry (Tsim Sha Tsui)

You'll find simple, contemporary and comfortable styles, much like a slightly hipper Gap, in this chain of modish boutiques. There are almost two dozen outlets throughout the territory.

🍴 EAT

🍴 AQUA
Italian, Japanese $$$

☎ 3427 2288; 29th fl, One Peking, 1 Peking Rd, Tsim Sha Tsui; 🕙 noon-11.30pm; Ⓜ Tsim Sha Tsui

This ultraminimalist place, just below a fabulous bar called Aqua Spirit, has a split personality, made up of Aqua Roma and Aqua Tokyo. The food is fine, but the views are simply astonishing.

🍴 CHANG WON KOREAN RESTAURANT 莊園韓國料理
Korean $$

☎ 2368 4606; 1G Kimberley St; 🕙 11.30am-midnight; Ⓜ Tsim Sha Tsui

If you're looking for truly authentic Korean food, head for this place, just one of several restaurants along a stretch that makes up Tsim Sha Tsui's 'Little Korea'. Try the excellent *bibimbab* (vegetables in sauce atop rice; $100).

🍴 DAN RYAN'S CHICAGO GRILL *American* $$$

☎ 2735 6111; Shop 315, 3rd fl, Ocean Terminal, Harbour City, Canton Rd, Tsim Sha Tsui; 🕙 11am-midnight Mon-Fri, 10am-midnight Sat & Sun; Ⓜ Tsim Sha Tsui 🚢 Star Ferry (Tsim Sha Tsui)

The theme at Dan Ryan's is 'Chicago', including a model elevated rail system overhead and jazz and big-band music on the sound system. It is also one of the best places for burgers and ribs in Hong Kong.

🍴 EASTERN PALACE CHIU CHOW RESTAURANT
東饗閣潮州酒家
Chiu Chow $$$

☎ 2730 6011; Shop 308, 3rd fl, Marco Polo Hong Kong Hotel, 3 Canton Rd, Tsim Sha Tsui; 🕙 10.30am-10.30pm; Ⓜ Tsim Sha Tsui

Some of the best Chiu Chow–style dim sum is served at this large hotel restaurant from 11am to 4pm daily. Try also the crab and shrimp balls, as well as the sliced goose in vinegar.

🍴 FAT ANGELO'S
Italian-American $$$

☎ 2730 4788; 8 Minden Ave, Tsim Sha Tsui; ⏱ noon-midnight; Ⓜ Tsim Sha Tsui
Huge portions, free salads, unlimited bread, relatively low prices and no surprises are the keys to success at this chain of Italian-American restaurants.

🍴 FELIX
International, Fusion $$$

☎ 2315 3188; 28th fl, Peninsula Hotel Hong Kong, cnr Salisbury & Nathan Rds, Tsim Sha Tsui; ⏱ 6-10.30pm; Ⓜ Tsim Sha Tsui (exit E) 🚢 Star Ferry (Tsim Sha Tsui)
Felix has a fantastic setting. You're sure to pay as much attention to the views and the Philippe Starck–designed interior as the fusion food (think dishes like lobster nachos and Hoisin grilled ribs). Towering ceilings and copper-clad columns surround the art-deco tables, while the view from the men's room is almost beyond belief.

🍴 FOOK LAM MOON 福臨門
Cantonese $$$

☎ 2366 0286; Shop 8, 1st fl, 53-59 Kimberley St; ⏱ 11am-11pm; Ⓜ Tsim Sha Tsui
Cheongsam-clad hostesses will guide you through the extensive, expensive and ususual menu – think shark's fin, frog, abalone. The pan-fried lobster balls are a house speciality. One of Hong Kong's top Cantonese restaurants.

🍴 GAYLORD 爵樂印度餐廳
Indian $$

☎ 2376 1001; 1st fl, Ashley Centre, 23-25 Ashley Rd, Tsim Sha Tsui; ⏱ noon-3pm & 6-11pm; Ⓜ Tsim Sha Tsui; Ⓥ
The dim lighting and live Indian music set the scene for enjoying the excellent rogan josh, dhal and other favourite dishes at Hong Kong's oldest Indian restaurant, which has been operating since 1972. There are lots of vegetarian choices as well.

🍴 GOOD SATAY *Malaysian* $

☎ 2739 9808; Shop 144-148, 1st fl, Houston Centre, 63 Mody Rd; ⏱ noon-10pm; Ⓜ Tsim Sha Tsui
This place on the 1st floor of a shopping and office complex doesn't look promising, but it serves some of the best (and most authentic) laksa and satay in town, as well as Hainan chicken rice ($39) that some diners travel here especially for. It's packed at lunch time.

🍴 HUTONG 胡同
Northern Chinese $$$

☎ 3428 8342; 28th fl, One Peking, 1 Peking Rd, Tsim Sha Tsui; ⏱ noon-3pm & 6pm-midnight; Ⓜ Tsim Sha Tsui 🚢 Star Ferry (Tsim Sha Tsui)
This very stylish Northern Chinese restaurant just below Aqua (opposite) is the best of both worlds: old-style furnishings and service,

International Japanese dining sensation Nobu has now set up shop in Tsim Sha Tsui

and modern food presentation and views. Try the wok-fried prawns with salty egg yolk and crab roe, or the Hutong-style crispy deboned lamb ribs. An award-winning stunner.

🍴 MERHABA 瑪哈巴
Turkish $$
☎ 2367 2263; Ground fl, Yiu Pont House, 12 Knutsford Tce, Tsim Sha Tsui; ⏱ 4pm-2am Mon-Thu, 4pm-3am Fri & Sat, 4pm-midnight Sun; Ⓜ Tsim Sha Tsui
This Turkish establishment with the exciting name of 'Hi' entertains with its Chinese belly dancer (Tuesday to Saturday). As always at Turkish restaurants, it would behove you to stick with the meze and the *raki* (anis-flavoured aperitif) and eschew the main courses.

🍴 NADAMAN 灘萬日本料理
Japanese $$$
⏱ 2733 8751; Basement 2, Kowloon Shangri-La, 64 Mody Rd, Tsim Sha Tsui East; ⏱ noon-3pm & 6.30-11pm; Ⓜ Tsim Sha Tsui
The authentic Japanese food at this restaurant has won it a well-deserved reputation. The set dinner ($440 to $1300) will make you very happy indeed if you're feeling expansive. Though it is expensive, it's worth it, and the lunch set menus ($120 to $480) are very good value.

🍴 NOBU *Japanese* $$$
⏱ 2721 1211; 2nd fl, Hotel InterContinental Hong Kong, 18 Salisbury Rd, Tsim Sha Tsui; ⏱ noon-2.30pm & 6-11.30pm; Ⓜ Tsim Sha Tsui

Japanese food with an international twist made for the global jet set, who dine here and at the other outlets of this ultra high-end chain in London, New York and Los Angeles. The world-famous *tiradito* (scallop, white fish, live octopus or razor clam) with spicy lime dressing that highlights the seafood and the black cod *saikyo yaki* (black cod in sweet miso) are all present and correct.

🍴 SABATINI *Italian* $$$

☎ 2733 2000; 3rd fl, Royal Garden Hotel, 69 Mody Rd, Tsim Sha Tsui East; ⏲ noon-2.30pm & 6-11pm; Ⓜ Tsim Sha Tsui 🚢 Tsim Sha Tsui East Ferry Pier 🚌 5, 8
Fine food and elegant surrounds (think frescoes and terracotta tiles) give Sabatini that classic Italian feel. Traditional offerings, such as fettuccine carbonara, are light in the best possible sense, leaving room to sample the exquisite desserts. The wine list is excellent but expensive.

🍴 WU KONG SHANGHAI RESTAURANT 滬江飯店
Shanghainese $$

☎ 2366 7244; Basement, Alpha House, 27-33 Nathan Rd, Tsim Sha Tsui; ⏲ 11.30am-midnight; Ⓜ Tsim Sha Tsui
The specialities at this Shanghainese restaurant – cold pigeon in wine sauce and crispy fried eels – are worth a trip across town. Dim sum is served all day.

🍴 YUMMY VIETNAMESE RESTAURANT 味佳居
Vietnamese $

☎ 3520 4343; 9th fl, Canton Plaza, 82-84 Canton Rd, Tsim Sha Tsui; ⏲ 11am-11.30pm; Ⓜ Tsim Sha Tsui
Don't worry about the fast-food canteen look, this is a truly authentic Vietnamese restaurant serving a range of dishes, from duck foetus egg ($18), or a satisfying bowl of pho (from $25), or roasted pigeon in lemongrass ($60).

🍸 DRINK

In general, Kowloon has more of a local Chinese scene than Hong Kong Island. There are four basic clusters of bars in Tsim Sha Tsui: along Ashley Rd; within the triangle formed by Hanoi Rd, Prat Ave and Chatham Rd; up along Knutsford Tce, Kowloon's tame answer to Lan Kwai Fong; and most recently along Minden Ave behind the Holiday Inn. Further towards Tsim Sha Tsui East it's mainly hostess-bar territory.

🍸 BAR *Bar*

⏲ 2315 3163; 1st fl, Peninsula Hotel Hong Kong, cnr Salisbury & Nathan Rds, Tsim Sha Tsui; ⏲ 5pm-2am Mon-Wed, 5pm-3am Thu-Sun; Ⓜ Tsim Sha Tsui (exit E) 🚢 Star Ferry (Tsim Sha Tsui)
For mellow 1940s and '50s jazz, take your smoking jacket along

and sip cognac at the Peninsula's most stylish watering hole. Your fellow tipplers will be serious business types, coutured couples and new money trying to look old(er).

Y BIERGARTEN *Pub*

☎ 2721 2302; 5 Hanoi Rd, Tsim Sha Tsui; ◷ noon-2am, happy hr 4-9pm; Ⓜ Tsim Sha Tsui

This clean modern place has a hits (and misses) jukebox and Bitburger on tap. It's popular with visiting Germans and others hankering after Black Forest ham, pork knuckle and sauerkraut. On fine days the front is open to the street.

Y CHILLAX *Bar*

☎ 2722 4338; 8 Minden Ave, Tsim Sha Tsui; ◷ 6pm-3am Mon-Sat; Ⓜ Tsim Sha Tsui

This tiny space lit by candles, patronised mainly by young locals, is good for simply sitting, slumping and generally 'chillaxing' from a

---

A VERY CLOSE SHAVE

Among the oft-told tales about the hotel affectionately known as 'the Pen' is the one about the spy with the razor. After the capitulation of British forces in Hong Kong to the Japanese on Christmas Day 1941, it was learned that the manager of the hotel barbershop had been a Japanese spy (and naval commander to boot), taking advantage of the chatty, informal atmosphere of the surrounds to collect useful information about the troop movements and so on.

---

day spent dodging through Tsim Sha Tsui. Things get more lively later when the DJ gets going.

Y FELIX *Bar*

☎ 2315 3188; 28th fl, Peninsula Hotel Hong Kong, cnr Salisbury & Nathan Rds, Tsim Sha Tsui; ◷ 6pm-2am; Ⓜ Tsim Sha Tsui (exit E) ⚓ Star Ferry (Tsim Sha Tsui)

Enjoy the fabulous view at this Philippe Starck–designed bar connected to Felix (p117) restaurant, one of the swankiest dining rooms in Hong Kong's poshest hotel. Guys, brace yourselves for a dramatic view through the gents' urinals.

Y LOBBY LOUNGE

九龍香格里拉大酒店大堂酒廊 *Bar*

☎ 2721 1211; Hotel InterContinental Hong Kong, 18 Salisbury Rd, Tsim Sha Tsui; Ⓜ Tsim Sha Tsui

Felix might edge the magnificent Lobby Lounge for harbour views, but not by much, and this is a more spacious and relaxing space to take time to chat, enjoy cocktails and stare through those soaring plate-glass windows at the evening Hong Kong Island light show.

Y SKY LOUNGE *Bar*

☎ 2369 1111; 18th fl, Sheraton Hong Kong Hotel & Towers, 20 Nathan Rd, Tsim Sha Tsui; ◷ 4pm-1am Mon-Thu, 4pm-2am Fri, 2pm-2am Sat, 2pm-1am Sun; Ⓜ Tsim Sha Tsui ⚓ Star Ferry (Tsim Sha Tsui)

Before you can pooh-pooh the departure-lounge feel of this long bar you'll have already started marvelling at the view. Don't take flight: sit down in a scoop chair, sip a drink and scoff international snacks.

⭐ PLAY

⭐ BAHAMA MAMA'S
Club

☎ 2368 2121; 4-5 Knutsford Tce, Tsim Sha Tsui; ⏱ 5pm-3am Sun-Thu, 5pm-4am Fri & Sat, happy hr 5-9pm; Ⓜ Tsim Sha Tsui

Mama's theme is tropical-island inspired and, unusually for most late-night watering holes, it's a friendly spot. On Friday and Saturday nights there's a DJ and a young crowd shaking their thing out on the postage-stamp-sized dance floor.

⭐ CLOUDNINE 九雲居
Karaoke Bar

☎ 2723 6383; 7 Minden Ave, Tsim Sha Tsui; ⏱ 6pm-3am Mon-Sat; Ⓜ Tsim Sha Tsui

If you want to find out what the local kids do of an evening (or at least those with some cash to burn), step through the egg-shaped doorway of this stylish little bar-cum-karaoke joint, take a seat and listen to Canto-pop classics get murdered.

⭐ HARI'S *Bar, Live Music*

☎ 2369 3111 ext 1345; Mezzanine, Holiday Inn Golden Mile, 50 Nathan Rd, Tsim Sha Tsui; ⏱ 5.30pm-2am, happy hr 5.30-9pm Mon-Sat, all evening Sun; Ⓜ Tsim Sha Tsui

Tacky, classy or neither? You decide after you've had a couple of speciality martinis (there are over a dozen to challenge you). There's live music nightly, from 6.15pm and again at 8.45pm Monday to Saturday, and from 7.30pm on Sunday.

⭐ HONG KONG CULTURAL CENTRE 香港文化中心
Concert Hall, Theatre

☎ 2734 2009; www.hkculturalcentre.gov.hk; 10 Salisbury Rd, Tsim Sha Tsui; tickets $100-500; Ⓜ Tsim Sha Tsui (exit E) 🚢 Star Ferry (Tsim Sha Tsui)

Clad in pink ceramic tiles and lacking a single window in one of the most dramatic spots on earth, this building's shell is an aesthetic stinker. However, inside you'll find Hong Kong's premier venue – with a 2000-seat concert hall with an impressive Rieger pipe organ, two theatres, rehearsal studios and a grand main lobby. It's home to the Hong Kong Philharmonic and the Hong Kong Chinese Orchestra, and major touring companies play here. There are daily tours (adult/child $10/5); phone ahead for bookings.

>KOWLOON: YAU MA TEI & MONG KOK

Just north of Tsim Sha Tsui the narrow byways of Yau Ma Tei (yow-ma-day; meaning 'Place of Sesame Plants') reward the explorer with a close-up look of a more traditional Hong Kong. The streets running east to west between Kansu St and Jordan Rd include Nanking St (mahjong shops and parlours), Ning Po St (paper kites and votives, such as houses, mobile phones and hell money, to burn for the dead) and Saigon St (herbalist shops, old-style tailors, pawnshops). On Shanghai St you'll find Chinese bridal and trousseau shops. Mong Kok (Prosperous Point) is one of Hong Kong's most congested working-class residential areas, as well as one of its busiest shopping districts. Traditionally the place locals came to buy everyday items, such as clothes, shoes, computer accessories and kitchen supplies, the area is rapidly getting a facelift, spurred on by the opening of the Langham Place Mall.

YAU MA TEI & MONG KOK

◉ SEE

◉ JADE MARKET 玉器市場
Kansu & Battery Sts, Yau Ma Tei; admission free; ⏱ **10am-6pm;** Ⓜ **Yau Ma Tei (exit C), Jordan (exit A)** 🚌 **9**
The jade knick-knacks, including Buddha charm necklaces and delicately carved zodiac animals, on sale at this market make great mementos and presents. The market is split into two parts by the loop formed by Battery St and has hundreds of stalls. Unless you really know your nephrite from your jadeite, though, it's not wise to buy expensive pieces here.

◉ SHANGHAI ST ARTSPACE 上海街視藝空間
☎ **2770 2157; 404 Shanghai St, Mong Kok; admission free;** ⏱ **11am-2pm & 3-8pm Tue-Sun;** Ⓜ **Yau Ma Tei (exit A1), Mong Kok (exit E1)**
Funded by the Hong Kong Arts Development Council, this exhibition hall is a small venue in an unusual location and concentrates on cutting-edge new art by local artists. Video assemblages, photography, computer art and mixed media all get coverage.

◉ TEMPLE ST NIGHT MARKET 廟街夜市
Temple St, Yau Ma Tei; admission free; ⏱ **4pm-midnight;** Ⓜ **Jordan (exit C2), Yau Ma Tei (exit C)**

Temple St, which extends from Man Ming Lane in the north to Nanking St in the south and is cut in two by the Tin Hau temple complex, is the place to go for cheap clothes, *dai pai dong* (open-air street stalls) food, Chinese memorabilia, watches, pirate CDs and DVDs, fake labels, footwear, cookware and everyday items. Any marked prices should be considered mere suggestions – this is definitely a place to bargain. It's also a place to catch some entertainment (p25).

◉ TIN HAU TEMPLE 天后廟
☎ **2332 9240; cnr Public Square St & Nathan Rd, Yau Ma Tei; admission free;** ⏱ **8am-5pm;** Ⓜ **Yau Ma Tei (exit C)**
A couple of blocks northeast of the Jade Market (left) is this temple, dedicated to Tin Hau, the

A CONSUMER HEAVEN IN HELL
In the more old-fashioned streets of Kowloon and Sheung Wan, you'll find clusters of shops selling paper votive offerings that are burned for the dead. The most popular are Hell bank notes, handy currency for the departed, but you can also buy them other little things to make eternity that bit more comfortable: paper Big Mac meals, cameras, Rolexes and, of course, that Hong Kong essential item, the mobile phone.

Find trinkets and talismans at the Jade Market

goddess of seafarers. You'll find a row of fortune tellers, some of whom speak English, if you head through the last doorway on the right from the main entrance on Public Square St. To buy and light one of the incense spirals you see hanging from the ceiling (they last 10 days) costs a mere $130.

☺ TUNG CHOI ST (LADIES') MARKET 通菜街(女人街)

Tung Choi St, Mong Kok; admission free; ⏰ noon-10.30pm; Ⓜ Mong Kok (exit D3)
Also known as Ladies' Market, the Tung Choi St market is a cheek-by-jowl affair offering up cheap clothes and trinkets. Vendors start setting up their stalls as early as

noon, but it's best to get here between 1pm and 6pm when there's much more on offer. Beware, the sizes stocked here tend to suit the lissom Asian frame. See also p25.

☺ YUEN PO ST BIRD GARDEN & FLOWER MARKET 園圃街雀鳥花園及花墟

Yuen Po St, Mong Kok; admission free; ⏰ 7am-8pm; Ⓜ Prince Edward (exit B1) 🚆 Mong Kok MTR East Rail 🚌 1, 1A, 2C, 12A
There are hundreds of birds for sale at the Yuen Po St Bird Garden, between Boundary St and Flower Market Rd, along with elaborate teak and bamboo birdcages (see boxed text, p127). If you carry on walking south along Yuen Po St, you'll reach the daily flower market, where some 50 florists sell blooms and plants. To see the flower market at its busiest, head there after 10am, especially on Sunday.

🛍 SHOP

Streets specialising in just one or two types of goods abound in Mong Kok and Yau Ma Tei. Fife St, for example, has an amazing collection of stalls selling old vinyl, books, ceramics, machinery and music scores. The northern end of Tung Choi St, on the other hand,

Kubrick Bookshop Café in Yau Ma Tei devotes its shelf space to all things film-related

is awash in shops selling goldfish (useful for soaking up bad feng shui) and bicycles. The street markets in Yau Ma Tei and Mong Kok also have the cheapest clothes in town.

⬚ LANGHAM PLACE MALL
朗豪坊商場 Mall
☎ 3520 2800; 8 Argyle St, Mong Kok; ⏱ 10am-11pm; Ⓜ Mong Kok
If you have not already had your fill of malls, this modern, 15-storey one with a massive, light-filled atrium has 300 stores, most of them brand-name clothes shops. Striking visuals are projected onto the 'Digital Sky' ceiling at the top of the mall.

⬚ MONG KOK COMPUTER CENTRE 旺角電腦中心
Computers
8-8A Nelson St, Mong Kok; Ⓜ Mong Kok
Three floors of computer shops. Though geared more towards the Cantonese-speaking market than the foreign one, you can generally get better deals here than in Tsim Sha Tsui. Check Winframe System (☎ 2300 1238; Shop 106-107, 1st fl).

⬚ TRENDY ZONE 潮流特區
Clothing & Accessories
Chow Tai Fook Centre, 580A Nathan Rd, Mong Kok; Ⓜ Mong Kok
This micromall is one of the most successful in Hong Kong and is

full of tiny shops selling new and vintage gear for guys and gals. **Rag Brochure** (☎ 2391 4660; Shop 4, basement; 🕑 1.30-10pm) is one of its better shops.

🏬 YUE HWA CHINESE PRODUCTS EMPORIUM

裕華國貨 *Department Store*

☎ 3511 2222; www.yuehwa.com; 301-309 Nathan Rd, Yau Ma Tei; 🕑 10am-10pm; Ⓜ Jordan

This cavernous place offers pretty much everything that a visiting souvenir hunter could ask for – seven packed floors of ceramics, furniture, souvenirs and clothing, as well as bolts of silk, herbs, clothes, porcelain, luggage, umbrellas and kitchenware. It's the biggest and best of some 18 branches of Yue Hwa across Hong Kong.

SINGING FOR LUCK

The Chinese have long favoured songbirds as pets, and a bird's singing prowess will often determine its price. Some species of birds are also considered harbingers of good fortune, which is why you'll sometimes see them being taken to the races. Enthusiasts gathering at the Yuen Po St Bird Garden (p125) in Mong Kok can often be seen feeding their caged prizes grasshoppers and other juicy insect treats through the bars of the cages with chopsticks.

🍴 EAT

🍴 GOOD HOPE NOODLE

好旺角粥麵家 *Noodle Bar* $

☎ 2394 5967; 146 Sai Yeung Choi St South, Mong Kok; 🕑 11am-3am; Ⓜ Mong Kok

This busy noodle stop is known far and wide for its terrific wonton soups and shredded pork noodles with spicy bean sauce. It's an eat-and-go sort of place, so don't come here if you feel like lingering.

🍴 KUBRICK BOOKSHOP CAFÉ

Café $

☎ 2384 5465; Shop H2, Prosperous Garden, 3 Public Square St, Yau Ma Tei; 🕑 11.30am-10pm; Ⓜ Yau Ma Tei

This café and bookshop next to the Broadway Cinematheque (p129) has a great range of film-related books, magazines and paraphernalia, and serves good coffee and decent pre-flick food, such as sandwiches ($33 to $42) and pasta dishes ($35 to $45).

🍴 MIDO 美都餐室

Hong Kong Fast Food $

☎ 2384 6402; 63 Temple St, Yau Ma Tei; 🕑 7.30am-10pm; Ⓜ Yau Ma Tei

This ultimate version of a *cha chan tang,* a uniquely Hong Kong café with local dishes, in a 1950s building opposite the Tin Hau Temple (p124) serves meals throughout the day, but it's best to come at

NEIGHBOURHOODS

KOWLOON: YAU MA TEI & MONG KOK

Catch an art-house flick at the Broadway Cinematheque

breakfast ($15 to $30) or in the afternoon for such oddities as *yuan yang* (equal parts coffee and black tea with milk), *ling lok* (boiled cola with lemon and ginger) and toast smeared with condensed milk. See also p25.

🍴 MING COURT 明閣
Cantonese $$$
☎ 3552 3388; 6th fl, Langham Place Hotel, 555 Shanghai St, Mong Kok; ☾ 11am-3pm & 6-10.30pm; Ⓜ Mong Kok

This restaurant in the flash Langham Place Hotel serves excellent modern Cantonese fare in a lovely dining room surrounded by replicas of ancient pottery unearthed in the area. Dim sum is served at lunch daily.

🍴 MIU GUTE CHEONG VEGETARIAN RESTAURANT
Vegetarian, Indian $
☎ 2771 6218; 31 Ning Po St, Yau Ma Tei; ☾ 11am-11pm; Ⓜ Jordan; Ⓥ

Cheap, cheerful and family-friendly. The tofu is fresh and firm, the vegetables are the pick of the market and the tea flows freely. Takeaway dim sum is $3 to $6.

🍴 SAINT'S ALP TEAHOUSE
仙跡岩 *Chinese Snacks* $
☎ 2782 1438; 61A Shantung St, Mong Kok; ☾ 11.30am-12.30am Sun-Thu, 11.30am-1am Fri & Sat; Ⓜ Mong Kok

One in a chain of clean and very cheap snackeries in Hong Kong (look for the footprint logo). It's a great pit stop for some exotic Taiwanese-style frothy tea with tapioca drops and Chinese snacks such as shrimp balls, noodles and rice puddings.

🍴 YAGURA *Japanese* $$

☎ 2710 1010; Lower ground fl, Eaton Hotel, 380 Nathan Rd, Kowloon; ⏰ noon-3pm & 6pm-midnight; Ⓜ Jordan

Terrific Japanese food covering most bases, including sushi, tempura and yakitori, at pretty sensible prices. Try the grilled live scallops.

⭐ PLAY

◻ BROADWAY CINEMATHEQUE
百老匯電影中心 *Cinema*

☎ 2388 3188; www.cinema.com.hk; Ground fl, Prosperous Garden, 3 Public Square St, Yau Ma Tei; tickets $32-55; Ⓜ Yau Ma Tei

Yau Ma Tei may seem like an unlikely place for an alternative cinema, but it's worth checking out for new art-house releases and re-runs here. The Kubrick Bookshop Café (p127) next door serves good coffee and light bites.

>KOWLOON: NEW KOWLOON

Before high-rises give way to mountains and scrub, you'll find the so-called New Kowloon (no one in town uses this purely administrative phrase). A sprawling conurbation and a slice of unvarnished Hong Kong urban living, the area contains two of Hong Kong's most prestigious seats of learning, the Hong Kong Baptist University and City University of Hong Kong, as well as many of the city's bridal shops, where brides to be can choose their finery and even perform the ceremony itself. It's not a beautiful part of town and lacks the glamour of the central districts, but there are some worthwhile places of interest worth seeking out, including a serenely beautiful nunnery, and the most vibrant temple in Hong Kong. Most places of interest lie along the MTR stations of (from west to east) Sham Shui Po, Kowloon Tong, Lok Fu, Wong Tai Sin and Diamond Hill.

NEW KOWLOON

⊙ SEE

🛍 SHOP

🍽 EAT

SEE

CHI LIN NUNNERY
志蓮淨苑

☎ 2354 1604; 5 Chi Lin Dr, Diamond Hill; admission free; 🕙 nunnery 9am-5pm, garden 6.30am-7pm; Ⓜ Diamond Hill (exit C2, then 5min walk along Fung Tak Rd)

This Tang-style wooden complex, built in 1998 without a single nail, is a serene place with lotus ponds, bonsai, and silent nuns delivering offerings to Buddha and arhats (Buddhist disciples freed from the cycle of birth and death). Designed to show the harmony of humans with nature, the complex is a visual, architectural and spiritual balm amid the severe high-rises nearby.

KOWLOON WALLED CITY PARK
九龍寨城公園

☎ 2716 9962; www.lcsd.gov.hk/parks/ kwcp/en; Tung Tsing Rd, Kowloon City; admission free; 🕙 6.30am-11pm; Ⓜ Lok Fu (exit B, then 15min walk south on Junction & Tung Tau Tsuen Rds) 🚌 1, 10, 113

The walls that enclose this beautiful park were once the perimeter of a notorious village that technically remained part of China throughout British rule. The

Chi Lin Nunnery makes a striking contrast to the city's skyscrapers

HONG KONG'S OWN BLOSSOM

The flower on Hong Kong's flag is the *Bauhinia blakeana*, also called the Hong Kong orchid. This species of bauhinia exists nowhere else. From early November to March you may see the purple blossoms on bauhinia trees, a species unique to the territory, in Victoria Park (p92), Kowloon Walled City Park (opposite) or outside the Foreign Correspondent Club (Map p55, D4) in Central.

enclave was known for its vice, prostitution, gambling and – worst of all – illegal dentists. In 1984 the Hong Kong government acquired the area, rehoused the residents, bulldozed the tenements and replaced them with pavilions, ponds, turtles, goldfish and exquisite flora in this attractive park.

☯ SIK SIK YUEN WONG TAI SIN TEMPLE
嗇色園黃大仙祠

☎ 2854 4333; Lung Cheung Rd, Wong Tai Sin; donation requested; ◷ 7am-6pm; Ⓜ Wong Tai Sin (exit B2)

A sensory whirl of colourful pillars, roofs, lattice work, flowers and incense, this busy and hugely atmospheric temple is a destination for all walks of Hong Kong society, from pensioners to businessmen, parents and young professionals. Some come simply to pray,

others to divine the future with *chim*, bamboo 'fortune sticks' that are shaken out of a box on to the ground and then read by a fortune teller (they're available for free to the left of the main temple). For more see the boxed text, below, and p20.

🛍 SHOP

🛍 GOLDEN COMPUTER ARCADE 黃金電腦商場
Computers

Basement & 1st fl, 146-152 Fuk Wa St, Sham Shui Po; Ⓜ Sham Shui Po

The cramped stalls inside are pretty much the cheapest places in Hong Kong for computers and components as well as cheap software and accessories, such as keyboards,

STICKY FORTUNES

There are any number of props and implements that Chinese use to predict the future, but the most popular method of divination in Hong Kong is with the *chim* (fortune sticks), found at Buddhist and Taoist temples, including Sik Sik Yuen Wong Tai Sin Temple (left). The sticks are shaken out of a box on to the ground; each bears a numeral corresponding to a printed slip of paper in a set held by the temple guardian. That slip of paper should be taken to the temple's fortune teller, who can interpret its particular meaning for you.

Head to Kowloon Walled City Park (p132) to enjoy some tranquillity away from the city's hectic centre

ink cartridges, CDs and DVDs. Most shops open daily from 10am to 10pm but some don't open until noon. It's packed on weekends.

🍴 EAT

The neighbourhood of Kowloon City is Hong Kong's Thai quarter, and it's worth a journey if you're looking for a *tom yum* (Thai hot and sour soup) or green-curry fix. The surrounding neighbourhood is packed with herbalists, jewellers, tea merchants and bird shops; it's worth having a postprandial meander to take a look.

🍴 FRIENDSHIP THAI FOOD
Thai $
☎ 2382 8671; 38 Kai Tak Rd, Kowloon City; 🕒 3pm-midnight; 🚌 5C, 101

Among the simplest and most authentic of the restaurants, Friendship Thai Food attracts Thai maids by the mop and bucketful.

🍴 GOLDEN ORCHARD THAI RESTAURANT *Thai* $
☎ 2383 3076; 12 Lung Kong Rd, Kowloon City; 🕒 noon-midnight; 🚌 5C, 101
Close to Friendship Thai Food, this eatery has spill-over rooms for when its restaurant fills up.

🍴 WONG CHUN CHUN THAI RESTAURANT *Thai* $
☎ 2716 6269; Ground & 1st fl, Belshine Centre, 23 Tak Ku Ling Rd, Kowloon City; 🕒 11am-2am; 🚌 5C, 101
One of the largest restaurants in Kowloon City and keeps later hours than most of its competition.

>NEW TERRITORIES

Along with Lantau, the New Territories contain the rural and wild places of Hong Kong. Given the very close proximity of seven million people that might sound an odd claim, but you really can get away from the city in the New Territories (so called because the land was leased to Britain in 1898, half a century after Hong Kong Island and Kowloon). Extensive country parks, including the spectacular and unspoiled Sai Kung Peninsula, are not the only appeal of the sprawling area bordering China proper. A world-class museum, one of Hong Kong's most interesting monasteries and a new wetland centre are among the other worthwhile attractions in this diverse chunk of Hong Kong. Getting to and around the New Territories is easy. The area is well served by the main east and west rail lines, by light rail services in the west, and a regular and reliable bus network. Taxis are plentiful and catching one from the main towns and stations to go the last kilometre or so to a place of interest is a worthwhile and relatively inexpensive investment.

NEW TERRITORIES

NEIGHBOURHOODS

NEW TERRITORIES

👁 SEE

👁 HONG KONG HERITAGE MUSEUM 香港文化博物館

☎ 2180 8188; www.heritagemuseum .gov.hk; 1 Man Lam Rd, Sha Tin; adult/ child $10/5, free Wed; 🕙 10am-6pm Mon & Wed-Sat, 10am-7pm Sun; 🚈 Sha Tin MTR East Rail, then 10min walk west & south along Tai Po & Lion Rock Tunnel Rds

If you only visit one museum in Hong Kong, make it this award-winning, three-storey purpose-built innovator with magnificent displays on Cantonese opera and the cultural heritage of the New Territories, the Children's Discovery Gallery (which has learning and play zones) and a gallery for the impressive art collection of one Dr TT Tsui.

👁 HONG KONG WETLAND PARK 香港濕地公園

☎ 3152 2666, 2708 8885; www.wetland park.com; Wetland Park Rd, Tin Shui Wai; adult/child $30/15; 🕙 10am-5pm Wed-Mon; 🚈 MTR West Rail to Tin Shui Wai then Light Rail 705 or 706, 🚌 967

This 61-hectare park in Tin Shui Wai, north of Tuen Mun, focuses on the wetland ecosystems and biodiversity of the northwest New Territories. It's a wonderful place to spend an entertaining (and educational) morning or afternoon (p26). Bus 967 from the Admiralty MTR bus station on Hong Kong Island also serves the park.

Golden touch: Ten Thousand Buddhas Monastery

👁 SAI KUNG 西貢

Ⓜ Choi Hung, then minibus 1A or 1M, 🚌 92, 🚈 Sha Tin MTR East Rail, then bus 299

Apart from the Outlying Islands, the Sai Kung Peninsula is one of the last havens left in Hong Kong for hikers, swimmers and boaters, and most of it is one huge 7500-hectare country park. A short journey to any of the islands off Sai Kung town is rewarding. Hidden away are some excellent beaches that can be visited by *kaido* (small boats), which depart from the waterfront. The MacLehose Trail, a 100km route across the New Territories, begins at Pak Tam Chung on the Sai Kung Peninsula. On top of this, Sai Kung town boasts excellent bars and restaurants (right), especially along the attractive waterfront.

◉ TEN THOUSAND BUDDHAS MONASTERY 萬佛寺

☎ 2691 1067; Sha Tin; admission free; ⏲ 9am-5pm; ⓡ Sha Tin MTR East Rail

Built in the 1950s, this large complex actually contains more than 10,000 Buddhas – some 12,800 miniature statues line the walls of the main temple, in fact. Dozens of life-sized golden statues of Buddha's followers flank the steep steps leading to the monastery complex. There is also a nine-storey pagoda. The monastery sits atop Po Fook Hill about 500m northwest of Sha Tin MTR East Rail station. Take exit B and walk down the ramp. Turn left onto Pai Tau St and then right onto Sheung Wo Che St. At the end of this road, a series of signs in English will direct

you to the left along a concrete path to the first of some 400 steps up to the complex. Also see boxed text, left.

🍽 EAT

🍽 CRYSTAL JADE LA MIAN
翡翠拉麵小籠包

Shanghainese $$

☎ 2699 9220; 1st fl, New Town Plaza Phase I, Sha Tin; ⏲ noon-3pm & 6-11.30pm; ⓡ Sha Tin MTR East Rail

Tasty and creditable *xiao long bao* (dumplings in soup), a Shanghai speciality, is the reason for coming. Try the beef stew and dumplings with chilli oil.

🍽 DIA *Indian* $$

☎ 2791 4466; Shop 2, block A, ground fl, 42-56 Fuk Man Rd, Sai Kung; ⏲ 11am-11pm; 🚌 92, 299

The stylish rattan and blue-satin surrounds and the fresh flavours of the mostly North Indian dishes attract a well-heeled crowd. Curries (moderately spicy) are the mainstay.

🍽 JASPA'S

International, Fusion $$

☎ 2792 6388; 13 Sha Tsui Path, Sai Kung; ⏲ 8.30am-midnight; 🚌 92, 299

Jaspa's is an upbeat, casual place serving international and fusion food to a motley crowd.

MIDAS TOUCH

The mummy under glass in the main temple of the Ten Thousand Buddhas Monastery (above) is the embalmed body of Yuet Kai (1878–1965), the monastery's founder. He was so revered that upon his death his corpse was encased in gold leaf. The box next to the bier collects donations for the temple's – and the Venerable Yuet's – upkeep.

>OUTLYING ISLANDS

Even if you're here for only a few days, try to make some time to see one or two of the islands. They offer a greener, slower-paced, less built-up side of Hong Kong compared to the teeming city centre. The largest, Lantau, is almost twice the size of Hong Kong Island, yet it is sparsely populated, offering great areas of wilderness, tranquil monasteries and long stretches of empty beach. Cheung Chau's winding streets afford an insight into a more traditional, low-rise way of life, while the car-free tracks of leafy Lamma Island lead to seafood restaurants and dramatic views from the ridge of its rocky spine. The islands listed here are all easily accessible from Hong Kong Island daily, and Cheung Chau and Lantau can be reached from Kowloon on the weekend as well.

OUTLYING ISLANDS

◐ SEE
Cheung Chau	1 D3
Cheung Po Tsai Cave	2 D4
Cheung Sha Beach	3 C3
Hong Kong Disneyland	4 E1
Kwun Yam Wan (Afternoon) Beach	5 D4
Lamma Island	6 F4

Lantau Trailhead	7 B3
Lantau Trailhead	8 C2
Ngong Ping Skyrail	(see 9)
Ngong Ping Village	9 B3
Pak Tai Temple	10 D4
Po Lin Monastery	(see 9)
Tai O	11 A3
Tian Tan Buddha	(see 9)

▯↾ EAT
Bookworm Café	12 F3
Hometown Teahouse	13 D4
Po Lin Vegetarian Restaurant	(see 9)
Rainbow Seafood Restaurant	14 F4
Stoep	15 C3

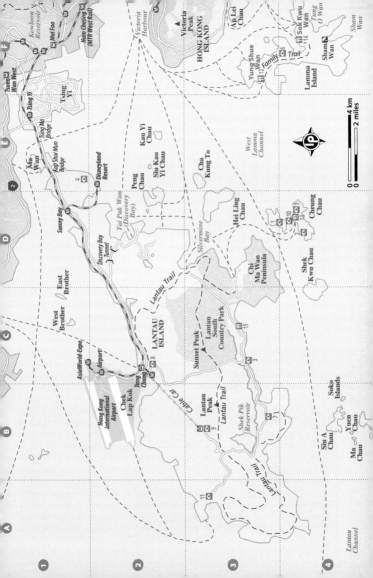

NEIGHBOURHOODS

OUTLYING ISLANDS

👁 SEE

🔘 CHEUNG CHAU 長洲

🚢 **Cheung Chau from Central (pier 5, Outlying Islands ferry terminal) or Tsim Sha Tsui (Star Ferry Pier, weekends only)**
The houseboats bobbing up and down Cheung Chau's busy harbour are one attraction here, but make sure you also see **Pak Tai Temple** (☎ 2981 0663; Pak She Fourth Lane; admission free; ⏰ 9am-5pm), site of the colourful Bun Festival (see below) in May, swim at **Kwun Yam Wan (Afternoon) Beach** (which is also popular with windsurfers) and visit **Cheung Po Tsai Cave** in the southwest corner, which was an old pirate hideout.

🔘 LAMMA ISLAND 南丫島

🚢 **Yung Shue Wan or Sok Kwu Wan from Central (pier 4, Outlying Islands ferry terminal) or Aberdeen**
The third-largest island after Lantau and Hong Kong, Lamma is known for its lively pubs, seafood restaurants, beaches and hikes. The laid-back lifestyle, strong feeling of community and relatively low rental costs make it a popular place with expats. Climbing the steep trails along the rocky spine of Lamma above Yung Shue Wan affords great views of the shipping lanes. An easier way to see a good portion of the island is to follow the 4km-long Family Trail between the two main villages, Yung Shue Wan and Sok Kwu Wan, which takes a little over an hour.

🔘 LANTAU ISLAND 大嶼山

🚢 **Mui Wo from Central (pier 6, Outlying Islands ferry terminal) or Tsim Sha Tsui (Star Ferry Pier, weekends only)**
More than half of Lantau's surface area is designated country parkland, and there are several superb mountain trails, including the 70km **Lantau Trail**, which passes over Lantau Peak (957m). There

BUN FIGHTS

If you're here in May, make for the bun towers built near Pak Tai Temple (above), an iconic part of the colourful eight-day Cheung Chau Bun Festival. The towers are formed from bamboo scaffolding up to 20m high and covered with sacred rolls. Formerly, people would scramble up the towers on the designated day to grab one of the buns for good luck, but the practice stopped after a fatal accident in 1978. The tower-climbing event has been resurrected as a race with extra safety precautions. On the third day of the festival (a Sunday), there's a lively procession of floats, stilt walkers and colourfully dressed 'floating children', who are carried through the streets on long poles cleverly wired to metal supports hidden under their clothing.

A welcoming sight – Tian Tan Buddha on Lantau

eral Buddhist-related multimedia attractions, including Walking with Buddha and Monkey's Tale Theatre (adult/child $65/35 for both), shops and food outlets, and served by the **Ngong Ping Skyrail** (adult/child one way $58/28, return $88/45; 🦽) cable car from Tung Chung. Lantau's newest attraction is **Hong Kong Disneyland** (☎ 830 830; www.hongkongdisneyland.com; adult/child Mon-Fri $295/210, Sat & Sun $350/250; ⏱ 10am-9pm Apr-Oct, 10am-7pm Nov-Mar; 🦽), located on the northeast coast and served by its own Mass Transit Rail (MTR) station. In truth, unless you have very young children in tow, Ocean Park (p102) on Hong Kong Island offers more interest and thrills than this rather lame branding exercise aimed at mainland Chinese visitors.

are also some excellent beaches, including long and empty **Cheung Sha**, some interesting traditional villages, such as **Tai O** (famous for its rope-tow ferry and pungent shrimp paste) and several important religious retreats, including the **Po Lin Monastery** (admission free; ⏱ 6am-6pm) and the striking, 23m **Tian Tan Buddha** (admission free; ⏱ 10am-5.30pm). Adjacent to the complex is **Ngong Ping Village** (☎ 2109 9179; www.np360.com.hk; admission free; ⏱ 10am-6pm Mon-Fri, 10am-6.30pm Sat & Sun; 🦽), with sev-

🍴 EAT

🍴 BOOKWORM CAFÉ
Vegetarian $

☎ 2982 4838; 79 Main St, Yung Shue Wan, Lamma Island; ⏱ 10am-9pm Mon-Fri, 9am-10pm Sat, 9am-9pm Sun; 🚢 Yung Shue Wan; Ⓥ

The Bookworm Café is not just a great vegetarian café-restaurant with fruit juices and organic wine, it's also a secondhand bookshop and an internet café. It's a very convivial spot.

TURTLE OUTRAGE

Sham Wan on Lamma's southern coast has traditionally been the one beach in the whole of Hong Kong where endangered green turtles (*Chelonia mydas*) still struggle onto the sand to lay their eggs from early June to the end of August. Along with developers, a major hurdle faced by the long-suffering turtles is the appetite of Lamma locals for their eggs. In 1994, three turtles laid about 200 eggs, which were promptly consumed by villagers. Today anyone taking, possessing or attempting to sell one of the eggs faces a fine of $100,000 and one year in prison.

🍴 HOMETOWN TEAHOUSE
故鄉茶寮 *Japanese, Café* $

☎ 2981 5038; 12 Tung Wan Rd, Cheung Chau; 🕐 noon-midnight; 🚢 Cheung Chau

This tiny, charming place run by an amiable Japanese couple serves simple, inexpensive lunches and dinners, but the afternoon tea – sushi, pancake, tea – is what you should come for.

🍴 PO LIN VEGETARIAN RESTAURANT 寶蓮苑素食
Vegetarian $

☎ 2985 5248; Ngong Ping village, Lantau Island; 🕐 11.30am-4.30pm; 🚢 Mui Wo, then bus 2; Ⓥ

This simple meatless restaurant on Lantau is located in the covered arcade to the left of the main Po Lin Monastery building. Buy your ticket at the monastery or at the ticket office below the Tian Tan Buddha statue. Sittings occur every 30 minutes.

🍴 RAINBOW SEAFOOD RESTAURANT
天虹海鮮酒家
Chinese, Seafood $$

☎ 2982 8100; Shops 1A & 1B, ground fl, 16-20 First St, Sok Kwu Wan, Lamma Island; 🕐 11am-10.30pm; 🚢 Sok Kwu Wan

The Rainbow, which has a couple of waterfront locations, specialises in seafood, especially steamed grouper, lobster and abalone.

🍴 STOEP
International, Mediterranean $

☎ 2980 2699; 32 Lower Cheung Sha Village, Lantau Island; 🕐 11am-10pm Tue-Sun; 🚢 Mui Wo, then bus 1 or 3

This Mediterranean-style restaurant, which has a huge terrace right on Lower Cheung Sha Beach, serves acceptable meat and fish dishes. Be sure to make book ahead on weekends if you want a taste of its flavours.

Enjoy a shady respite at the Lou Lim Ioc Garden (p149)

MACAU

MACAU

Not long ago a sleepy, Portuguese colony, tiny Macau has in a few short years become a 24/7 gambling megaresort. An hour's boat ride west of Hong Kong, this is China's Las Vegas, a brash, neon-lit magnet for mainland Chinese gamblers. Chunks of Nevada seem to have been helicoptered into the heart of its captivating fusion of Asian and Mediterranean cultures and heritage, creating an extraordinary mix of the paint-still-drying new and the centuries old. Four-and-a-half centuries of Portuguese rule up to 1999 (when China resumed sovereignty) are still written in the territory's older architecture: picture-postcard churches and civic buildings, narrow streets, traditional shops, and Portuguese and Macanese restaurants. The tiny (27.5 sq km) territory consists of the Macau Peninsula, which is attached to China, and across the bridges the 'islands', Taipa and Coloane (now a single land mass dominated by the huge new gambling epicentre of the Cotai Strip). Getting to Macau from Hong Kong has never been easier, with high-speed ferries running between the two territories every half-hour day and night.

MACAU

🅒 SEE
A-Ma Temple 1 A2
Chapel of St Francis
  Xavier 2 B6
Church of St Dominic 3 A2
Holy House of Mercy .... (see 4)
Largo do Senado 4 A2
Leal Senado 5 A2
Lou Lim loc Garden 6 B1
Macau Fisherman's
  Wharf 7 B2
Macau Museum 8 A1
Macau Tower 9 A2
Old Protestant
  Cemetery 10 A1

Ruins of the Church of
  St Paul 11 A1
Treasury of Sacred Art.. (see 3)

🍴 EAT
A Lorcha 12 A2
Café Nga Tim .... (see 16)
Caravela 13 A2
Clube Militar de
  Macau 14 A2
Corner's Wine Bar
  & Tapas Café .... (see 11)
Cozinha Pinócchio 15 B4
Espaço Lisboa 16 B6
Fernando 17 C6

Restaurante Litoral 18 A2
Tou Tou Koi 19 A2

🍸 DRINK
Vasco 20 B2
Whisky Bar 21 B2

⭐ PLAY
Casino Lisboa 22 A2
Emperor Palace
  Casino 23 A2
Grand Lisboa .... (see 22)
Venetian 24 B4
Wynn Macau
  Casino 25 A2

MACAU

MACAU PENINSULA

⊙ SEE

⊙ A-MA TEMPLE 媽閣廟

Templo de A-Ma; Rua de São Tiago da Barra; admission free; 🕙 **10am-6pm**
North of Barra Hill, this 17th-century temple is dedicated to the goddess A-Ma, who is better known in Hong Kong as Tin Hau. At the main entrance is a large boulder with a coloured relief of a *lorcha* (a traditional sailing vessel).

⊙ CHURCH OF ST DOMINIC 玫瑰堂

Igreja de São Domingos; Largo de São Domingos; admission free; 🕙 **8am-6pm**
Arguably the most beautiful in Macau, this 17th-century baroque church contains the **Treasury of Sacred Art** (Tesouro de Arte Sacra; ☎ 367 706; admission free; 🕙 10am-6pm), an Aladdin's cave of ecclesiastical art.

⊙ LARGO DO SENADO 議事亭前地

Avenida de Almeida Ribeiro
'Senate Square', with its wavy black-and-white cobblestones and beautiful colonial buildings, is the heart and soul of Macau, and is illuminated at night.

Lovely **Holy House of Mercy** (Santa Casa da Misericordia; ☎ 573 938; Travessa da Misericordia 2; admission $5; 🕙 10am-1pm & 2.30-5.30pm Mon-Sat), on the south-eastern side of the square, was a home for orphans and prostitutes in the 18th century. It's opposite Leal Senado.

⊙ LEAL SENADO 民政總署大樓

163 Avenida de Almeida Ribeiro; admission free; 🕙 **gallery 9am-9pm Tue-Sun, library 1-7pm Mon-Sat**
Macau's most important historical building, the 'Loyal Senate' now houses the mayor's office, an art gallery and the ornately furnished Senate Library. Above the entrance to the blue-tiled courtyard garden is a heraldic inscription dating from 1654 that refers to Macau's support during Spain's 60-year occupation of Portugal.

JUST THE FACTS

Passport You need it to visit Macau.
Telephone code ☎ 853
Currency Pataca (MOPS), which is divided into 100 avos. Hong Kong dollars are accepted everywhere.
Information Macau Government Tourist Office (Map p147, A2; MGTO; ☎ 2831 5566; www.macautourism .gov.mo; 9 Largo do Senado; 🕙 9am-6pm); ferry terminal branch (Map p147, B2; ☎ 2872 6416; 🕙 9am-10pm).

ⓒ LOU LIM IOC GARDEN
盧廉若公園

Jardim de Lou Lim Ioc; 10 Estrada de Adolfo de Loureiro; admission free; 6am-9pm

This wonderful garden has huge shade trees, lotus ponds, bamboo groves, grottoes and a bridge with nine turns to escape from evil spirits (who apparently can only move in straight lines). Locals use the park to practise t'ai chi or play traditional Chinese musical instruments.

ⓒ MACAU FISHERMAN'S WHARF 澳門漁人碼頭

Doca dos Pescadores de Macau; ☎ 8299 3300; www.fishermanswharf.com.mo; **cnr Avenida de Amizade & Avenida Doutor Sun Yat Sen; admission free;** 24hr

This kitsch 'theme park', built on 112 hectares of reclaimed land in the Outer Harbour, combines attractions, hotels, shops, arcade games, restaurants and, beneath the cone of that plastic volcano, a couple of thrill rides.

ⓒ MACAU MUSEUM
澳門博物館

Museu de Macau; ☎ 2835 7911; www .macaumuseum.gov.mo; **Praceta do Museu de Macau, Fortaleza do Monte; adult/child $15/8, free on 15th of month;** 10am-6pm Tue-Sun

Housed in 17th-century Monte Fort, this worthwhile museum tells

Tread the cobblestones of Largo do Senado

an engaging multimedia tale of the history of the hybrid territory of Macau and is perhaps the best introduction to its traditions and culture.

ⓒ MACAU TOWER
澳門旅遊塔

Torre de Macau; ☎ 2893 3339; www .macautower.com.mo; **Largo da Torre de Macau; observation decks adult/child $80/40, climbs & walks from $40;** 10am-9pm Mon-Fri, 9am-9pm Sat & Sun

At 338m, the views across Macau's islands and city centre from the observation decks of this needle-like structure are spectacular (smog permitting). If you're after some adrenaline thrills, head outside the observation deck for a range of hair-raising climbs and walks.

● OLD PROTESTANT CEMETERY

15 Praça de Luís de Camões; admission free; ⏱ **8.30am-5.30pm**

The last resting place of (mostly Anglophone) Protestants, the gravestones at this atmospheric spot offer some stone-carved insights into Macau's history. Among those interred here are Irish-born artist George Chinnery (1774–1852), who spent most of his adult life in Macau painting, and Robert Morrison (1782–1834), the first Protestant missionary to China and author of the first Chinese-English dictionary.

● RUINS OF THE CHURCH OF ST PAUL 大三巴牌坊

Ruinas de Igreja de São Paulo; Rua de São Paulo; admission free

The weathered facade and majestic stairway are all that remain of this church, which was designed by an Italian Jesuit and was built by exiled Japanese Christians in the early 17th century. However, with its wonderful statues, portals and engravings, some consider it to be the greatest monument to Christianity in Asia.

THIS WAY AROUND

For information on getting to and from Macau from Hong Kong, see p184. Central Macau is best explored on foot; taxis are cheap for attractions further afield. The *Macau Tourist Map*, available from any Macau Government Tourist Office branch, has a full list of bus routes.

🍴 EAT

🍴 A LORCHA 船屋餐廳

Portuguese $$

☎ **2831 3193; 289A Rua do Almirante Sérgio;** ⏱ **12.30-3pm & 6.30-11pm Wed-Mon**

The much loved 'Sailboat' restaurant facing the Inner Harbour northwest of Macau Tower has some of the best Portuguese food in Macau, including signature dishes, such as *feijoada* (pork-knuckle stew), as well as baked duck rice and pork-ear salad.

🍴 CARAVELA 金船

Pastries $

☎ **2871 2080; Ground fl, Kam Loi Bldg, 7 Pátio do Comandante Mata e Oliveira;** ⏱ **8am-10pm Mon-Sat**

This excellent *pastelaria* (pastry shop) – and hang-out of choice for Portuguese residents – just north of Avenida de Dom João IV is a bit tricky to find, but the delectable pastries and snacks make it worth the search.

🍴 CLUBE MILITAR DE MACAU
澳門陸軍俱樂部

Portuguese $$$

☎ 2871 4000; 975 Avenida da Praia Grande; ⏱ noon-3pm & 7-11pm

The Military Club is one of Macau's most distinguished colonial buildings and its Portuguese restaurant is as atmospheric as you'll find. The food is very good, if perhaps not the best in town.

🍴 CORNER'S WINE BAR & TAPAS CAFÉ

Mediterranean $

☎ 2848 2848; 3 Travessa de São Paulo; ⏱ café noon-3pm & 6-11pm daily, wine bar 3pm-midnight Thu & Sun, 3pm-1am Fri & Sat

This roof-top bar and tapas joint offers that rare thing in Macau: outdoor dining. It's got a great location just across from the Ruins of the Church of St Paul (opposite)

and serves decent tapas dishes. At night it's a perfect place to come for some chilled-out drinks amid soft lighting and soothing music.

🍴 RESTAURANTE LITORAL
海灣餐廳 *Macanese* $$

☎ 2896 7878; 261A Rua do Almirante Sérgio; ⏱ noon-3pm & 5.30-10.30pm

This is arguably the best Macanese restaurant on the peninsula, with superb duck and baked rice dishes.

🍴 TOU TOU KOI

Cantonese $$

☎ 2857 2629; 6-8 Travessa do Mastro; ⏱ 8am-3pm & 5pm-12am

Down the alley opposite the Pawnshop Museum you'll find traditional Cantonese dishes no longer found in many other Chinese restaurants. Among the range of sumptuous dishes is its signature deep-fried stuffed crab with shrimp.

SHOP WISE

The narrow streets of the Macau Peninsula contain bustling markets and traditional Chinese shops, good destinations if you're hunting for mementos of your visit. Rua de Madeira is a charming market street, with many shops selling carved Buddha heads and other religious items. Rua dos Mercadores, which leads up to Rua da Tercena, will lead you past tailors, wok sellers, tiny jewellery shops, incense and mahjong shops, and other traditional businesses. At the far end of Rua da Tercena, where the road splits, is a flea market where you can pick up baskets and other rattan ware, jade pieces and old coins. Great streets for antiques, ceramics and curios (such as traditional Chinese kites) are Rua de São Paulo, Rua das Estalagens and Rua de São António, and the lanes off them. Almost every casino complex, including the Wynn Macao and the Venetian, are stuffed with high-end boutiques and global brands. Most shops are open from 10.30am or 11am to 6pm or 7pm, with a one-hour lunch break some time between 12.30pm and 2pm.

🍸 DRINK

🍸 VASCO Bar

☎ 8793 3831; Ground fl, Mandarin Oriental, 956-1110 Avenida da Amizade; ⏰ 2pm-2am

This cool, quiet, softly lit haven offers respite from crowds, noise and glowing neon. In the afternoon it serves tapas-style afternoon tea and in the evenings there's some excellent live music (accomplished jazz singers or good lounge music typically).

🍸 WHISKY BAR Bar

☎ 2838 3838; 16th fl, StarWorld, Avenida da Amizade; ⏰ 11am-2am Sun-Thu, 11am-3am Fri-Sat

High up in the glitzy new StarWorld hotel and casino, this modern bar offers grand vistas across the peninsula to the Guia Lighthouse, plus a Filipino covers band and a lively atmosphere, but it must be said, not much of a whisky menu. Get a window seat.

⭐ PLAY

With an increasing emphasis on entertainment as well as gambling, Macau's casinos are trying to generate some Vegas-style glamour. So, even if you don't fancy playing the tables (in many the minimum bet is $100 or more, punters must be over 18 and properly dressed), it's worth taking a look around.

🎰 CASINO LISBOA Casino

☎ 2837 5111; www.hotelisboa.com; Lisboa Hotel, 2-4 Avenida de Lisboa; ⏰ 24hr

With its garish 1960s exterior and 'Chinese baroque' interior, Casino Lisboa is the best known in Asia.

A CHINESE VEGAS

Macau has long been a gambling resort but is only now discovering how to act like one, with a high rolling, high kicking future ahead of it and an increasing emphasis on entertainment as well as gambling. Cirque du Soleil has already put up its big top here and big names such as Celine Dion regularly jet in to perform. For spectacle, silliness and sometimes both go to:

Cotai Strip (Map p147, B4) For a glimpse of what's to come in Macau, have a look at the vast casino hotel complexes springing up as far as the eye can see.

Emperor Palace Casino (p154) For entertaining kitsch from the portraits of European royalty to the Buckingham Palace–style door sentries.

Venetian (Map p147, B4; ☎ 2882 8888; www.venetianmacao.com; Estrada da Baía de N Senhora da Esperança; ⏰ 24hr) For singing gondoliers who punt you along a faux-Venetian Canal.

Wynn Macau Casino (p154) For the huge globe, which opens every 10 minutes to reveal...well, go and see for yourself. Baffling but impressive.

Peter Gorton
Musician with local band Soler

Who are Soler? They are a cool band. A small icon of both Hong Kong and Macau. **So which is better: Hong Kong or Macau?** It depends what you want. There's more going on in Hong Kong right now. Better nightlife, bigger buzz. But Macau is changing and it's not all about the casinos. The arts and entertainment scene is getting better all the time. **Where should I go to see good live music?** The live music scene is getting better in both places but that's from a low base. There are a couple of underground festivals happening now in Hong Kong. The Fringe Club (p71) is a more established, mainstream music venue, mostly good for rock and jazz. **Why is it such a struggle for live musicians?** The problem with live music is the popularity of karaoke. Things are changing, though and people are appreciating live music more these days.

⊞ EMPEROR PALACE CASINO
Casino

☎ 2888 9988; www.grandemperor
.com; 299 Avenida Comercial de
Macau; 🕐 24hr

Close to Largo do Senado, the
quirky Emperor Palace Casino is a
kitsch fantasy of European
Imperial splendour. Its ostenta-
tious display of marble columns
and a golden pathway of 78
one-kilogram gold bricks are pure
feng shui in action, designed to
bring good fortune.

⊞ GRAND LISBOA
Casino

☎ 2838 2828; www.grandlisboa.com;
Avenida de Lisboa; 🕐 24hr

Packed with rare artworks and
precious stones inside, the lavish
and spectacular Grand Lisboa's
towering, flaming-torch-shaped
megastructure has become the
landmark you navigate the peninsula streets by.

⊞ WYNN MACAU CASINO
Casino

☎ 2888 9966; www.wynnmacau.com;
Rua Cidade de Sintra; 🕐 24hr

The Vegas-style Wynn Macau
Casino is arguably the most
upmarket of the lot, with every
game imaginable (up to $2500
minimum bet) and original Mat-
isse and Renoir paintings on the
premises.

TAIPA & COLOANE ISLANDS

👁 SEE

◉ CHAPEL OF ST FRANCIS XAVIER 聖方濟各教堂

Capela de São Francisco Xavier; Avenida
de Cinco de Outubro, Coloane; admission
free; 🕐 10am-8pm

This delightful little church on the
waterfront was built in 1928 to
honour St Francis Xavier. He had
been a missionary in Japan, and
Japanese Catholics still come to
Coloane to pay their respects.

🍴 EAT

🍴 CAFÉ NGA TIM
Macanese $$

☎ 2888 2086; 8 Rua Caetano,
Coloane; 🕐 noon-1am

We love the Sino-Portuguese food,
laid-back atmosphere, location
(opposite the Chapel of St Francis
Xavier) and prices at this place.
The food, such as salt-and-pepper
prawns or barbecued chicken, is
simple and traditional.

🍴 COZINHA PINÓCCHIO
木偶葡國餐廳 *Macanese* $$

☎ 2882 7128; 4 Rua do Sol, Taipa;
🕐 11.45am-11.45pm

Delight in the technicolour façade of the Chapel of St Francis Xavier

The place that launched the Taipa Village restaurant phenomenon, 'Pinocchio Kitchen' specialises in grilled fresh sardines, quail, pigeon and roast lamb.

🍴 ESPAÇO LISBOA
里斯本地帶餐廳
Portuguese $$$
☎ 2888 2226; 8 Rua dos Gaivotas, Coloane; ◷ noon-3pm & 6.30-10pm Tue-Fri, noon-10.30pm Sat & Sun
The 'Lisbon Space' restaurant in a renovated village house serves some of the most carefully prepared Portuguese dishes in Macau. Try the fish (swordfish, grouper etc) stewed in a *cataplana* (traditional copper pot), or the curried crab.

🍴 FERNANDO *Portuguese* $$
☎ 2888 2264; 9 Praia de Hác Sá, Coloane; ◷ noon-9.30pm
Famed for its simple, inexpensive seafood and idyllic waterfront location, Fernando has a devoted clientele and a pleasantly relaxed atmosphere – though it can get pretty crowded in the evening.

All that high-rise urban bustle you've seen from afar is just one side to Hong Kong. This is also a city with green escapes, wild ocean shores, diverse culinary options and cultural attractions. Locate the highlights of what this compelling city has to offer with this easy-to-use rundown of what makes Hong Kong such a memorable destination.

Grab a drink and take in the spectacular city skyline at Aqua (p116)

ACCOMMODATION

OK, so the first choice you need to make is whether to stay Hong Kong Island side or Kowloon side. Many of the cool sights await and much of the nightlife goes down on the Island, but Tsim Sha Tsui (p106) has much to recommend it, not least that amazing view of Hong Kong Island (plus a profusion of museums and galleries).

If you're on a tight budget, your options on the Island side are limited more or less to busy Causeway Bay (p90), which is great for parks and shopping but is hardly Hong Kong's beating social heart. Over the water, Tsim Sha Tsui is rammed with budget places, mostly tiny guesthouses, some in shabby tenement blocks. It's livelier, too.

For those seeking a mid-priced stay, Wan Chai (p78) on Hong Kong Island has plenty of midrange places, some at very reasonable rates. Tsim Sha Tsui and Kowloon (p122), however, offer by far the most bang for your midrange buck.

If you have cash, or an expense account to splash, Hong Kong really is your playground and the very acme of luxury can be yours. The finer hotels here really are up there with the best in the world, from the old-school charm of the Peninsula (p110) in Tsim Sha Tsui, to the sleek modernity of the Four Seasons, your average oligarch's home away from home. Just name it, helicopter airport transfers maybe, or shopping by Rolls Royce Phantom, your wish is the concierge's command.

Hong Kong's two accommodation high seasons are from March to April and October to November, though things can be tight around Chinese New Year (late January or February) as well. Outside these periods, rates drop (sometimes substantially) and little extras can come your way: room upgrades, late checkout, free breakfast and complimentary cocktails.

WEB RESOURCES

If you fly into Hong Kong without having booked accommodation, the **Hong Kong Hotels Association** (www.hkha.org) can secure you a deal of up to 50% off more than 90 midrange to high-end hotels. Local travel agent www .taketraveller.com can get you similar deals.

BEST DELUXE HOTELS
> Four Seasons Hotel Hong Kong (www .fourseasons.com)
> Grand Hyatt Hotel (pictured above; www.hongkong.hyatt.com)
> Island Shangri-La (www.shangri-la .com)
> Mandarin Oriental (www.mandarin oriental.com)
> Peninsula Hong Kong (www.penin sula.com)

BEST BOUTIQUE HOTELS
> Hotel LKF (www.hotel-lkf.com.hk)
> Jia (www.jiahongkong.com)
> The Fleming (www.thefleming.com)
> The Minden (www.theminden.com)

BEST FOR STYLE ON A BUDGET
> Bishop Lei International House (www .bishopleihtl.com.hk)
> Hotel Jen (www.hoteljen.com.hk)
> Ice House (www.icehouse.com.hk)
> Stanford Hillview Hotel (www .stanfordhillview.com)
> The Salisbury (www.ymcahk.org.hk)

BEST GUESTHOUSES & HOSTELS
> Alisan Guest House (http://home .hkstar.com/~alisangh)
> Booth Lodge (http://boothlodge .salvation.org.hk)
> Hong Kong Hostel (www.wangfat hostel.com.hk)
> Rent-a-Room (www.rentaroomhk.com)
> YWCA Building (www.ywca.org.hk)

ARCHITECTURE

Over the centuries Hong Kong has played host to everything from Tao temples and Qing dynasty forts to Victorian churches and Edwardian hotels. But Hong Kong's ceaseless cycle of deconstruction and rebuilding means that few structures have survived the wrecking ball, at least in the central parts of the city. The best places for pre-colonial Chinese architecture still extant are the ancestral halls and walled villages of the New Territories (p136) and Outlying Islands (p140). A good way to see these is on the organised tours run by the Hong Kong Tourism Board (p194). Central (p40) on Hong Kong Island is a good hunting ground for surviving colonial architecture, though Tsim Sha Tsui (p106) can boast a few classic examples. Needless to say, enthusiasts of modern architecture will have a field day here. Central and Wan Chai (p78) on Hong Kong Island are especially rich showcases for the modern and contemporary buildings.

BEST PRE-COLONIAL CHINESE BUILDINGS
> Tin Hau Temple (p92)
> Law Uk Folk Museum buildings (see the boxed text, p96)
> Kowloon Walled City Park buildings (p132)

BEST CONTROVERSIAL BUILDINGS
> Bank of China Tower (p42)
> Hongkong & Shanghai Bank (p44)
> Hong Kong Cultural Centre (p121)
> Jardine House (p44)
> Two International Finance Centre (p46)

BEST COLONIAL BUILDINGS
> Flagstaff House Museum of Tea Ware (p80)
> Former French Mission Building (p42)
> Former Marine Police Headquarters (p108)
> Legislative Council Building (p45)
> Murray House (pictured right; p102)

SNAPSHOTS

DRINKING

Drinking venues in Hong Kong fall into two main categories: buzzing bars jammed with revellers shouting over the music and each other in the main nightlife districts, and quieter, plush hotel bars with smooth service, sensational views and some elbow room. This 24/7 city doesn't really do cosy little neighbourhood bars or pubs unless you visit some of the remote island (p140) or New Territories (p136) destinations.

Lan Kwai Fong (p65) in Central and, increasingly, the streets spilling up from it towards Soho are the best areas for bars. The stomping grounds of expat and Chinese suits and professionals, it's full of life and revellers almost every night. Pubs in Wan Chai (p86) are cheaper and more relaxed, and those in Tsim Sha Tsui (p119) generally more local.

BEST STYLISH BARS & PUBS
> Dragon-I (pictured above; p67)
> Lobby Lounge (p120)
> Maya (p87)
> Red Bar (p53)

BEST FOR SEEING & BEING SEEN
> 2121 (p65)
> Soda (p67)
> Staunton's Wine Bar & Café (p69)

BEST FOR ATMOSPHERE
> Chillax (p120)
> Felix (p120)

> Gecko Lounge (p67)
> Red Bar (p53)
> The Pawn (p88)

BEST FOR GENEROUS HAPPY HOURS
> Delaney's (p87)
> Devil's Advocate (p87)
> Inn Side Out & East End Brewery (p99)

BEST FOR MEETING NONPOSEURS
> Barco (p66)
> Club 71 (p66)
> Yumla (p73)

FOOD

It is hard to have a conversation in Hong Kong without mentioning food, especially when many still greet each other by asking, 'Have you eaten yet?'. The vast majority of Hong Kong's 10,000-odd restaurants serve Chinese food, of course. Cantonese is by far the most popular Chinese cuisine in Hong Kong, but Chiu Chow, Shanghainese, Sichuanese and Northern Chinese are also widely available. Cantonese cuisine is famously fresh: there's an emphasis on freshly slaughtered meat (mostly pork and chicken) and seafood. Simple techniques such as steaming and stir-frying allow the ingredients to retain their delicate and well-balanced flavours (for information on dim sum, see p22). Chiu Chow cuisine makes liberal use of garlic, vinegar and sauces; it's famous for goose and seafood dishes. Shanghainese cooking uses a lot of salted and preserved foods and relies on stewing, braising and frying. Sichuanese is the most fiery, making great use of chillies and pungent peppercorns. Northern Chinese food uses a lot of oils (eg sesame and chilli) coupled with ingredients such as vinegar, garlic, spring onions, bean paste and dark soy sauce. Steamed bread, dumplings and noodles are preferred to rice, and lamb and mutton, seldom seen on other Chinese menus, are also popular.

The full range of international fare is on your doorstep, too: Italian, Japanese, Brit pub grub, French, Korean, Indian and Mediterranean food is all well represented across most price ranges. Central (p51) is the best pick for Western restaurants, especially Soho (p61), though you'll also find a fair few in Tsim Sha Tsui (p116).

BEST DIM SUM RESTAURANTS
> City Hall Maxim's Palace (p51)
> Lin Heung Tea House (p63)
> Luk Yu Tea House (p64)
> Yung Kee (p65)

BEST FOR LATE-NIGHT BITES
> 369 Shanghai Restaurant (p83)
> Good Luck Thai Food (p63)

BEST FOR CHINESE FOOD
> Da Ping Huo (p62)
> Eastern Palace Chiu Chow Restaurant (p116)
> Wu Kong Shanghai Restaurant (p119)
> Yung Kee (p65)

Top left Barbecued ducks ready to be enjoyed at Yung Kee (p65) **Above** Delectable dim sum at Luk Yu Tea House (p64)

WORKOUT OR PAMPER

Aside from walking, hiking and t'ai chi (pictured below), most activity options will be of the indoor variety. Several fitness club chains in Hong Kong allow short-term memberships for $150 to $200 a day, and both Kowloon Park (p110) and Victoria Park (p92) have swimming pools that are for leisure as well as laps. Yoga is also popular, stretching from the sweaty hot variety to the more meditation-based practices.

If you're after sedentary relaxation, massage and pampering treats, there are some amazing spas in the high-end hotels – notably the Four Seasons, the Peninsula (p110), the InterContinental and the Grand Hyatt – and in dedicated places in Central (p40).

BEST HOTEL SWIMMING POOLS
> Four Seasons (www.fourseasons.com)
> Grand Hyatt Hotel (www.hongkong .hyatt.com)
> Renaissance Harbour View Hotel (www.renaissancehotels.com)
> Royal Garden Hotel (www.rghk.com.hk)
> Royal Plaza Hotel (www.royalplaza .com.hk)

BEST FOR PAMPERING
> Elemis Day Spa (p70)
> Happy Foot Reflexology Centre (p71)
> Sense of Touch (p73)
> Yoga Plus (p73)

GAY & LESBIAN

The gay scene in Hong Kong, while not exactly underground, is somewhat muted. Even so, it has undergone quite a revolution over a few short years. It was only in 1991 that the Crimes (Amendment) Ordinance removed criminal penalties for homosexual acts between consenting adults over the age of 18. Since then gay groups have been lobbying for legislation to address the issue of discrimination on the grounds of sexual orientation. Despite these changes, however, Hong Kong Chinese society remains fairly conservative, and it can still be risky for gays and lesbians to come out to their family members or employers. Be sure to get hold of a copy of the free monthlies *Gmagazine* or the more comprehensive *Q Guide,* or log on to **GayStation** (www.gaystation.com.hk) or **Gay Hong Kong** (www.gayhk.com).

BEST FOR CLUBBING
> Club 97 (p69)
> FINDS (pictured above; p62)
> Propaganda (p73)

SNAPSHOTS

KIDS

With its mad cityscapes, Cantonese kids sporting Japanese-style fashions and spiky hair, thrill rides up mountains and dozens of novel ways to get around, Hong Kong is a great travel destination for kids. Food and sanitation is of a high standard, the locals make a big fuss of younger kids and the territory is jam-packed with things to entertain. As a starting point for ideas, get a copy of the Hong Kong Tourism Board's *Hong Kong Family Fun Guide* (www.discoverhongkong.com).

Business travellers and tourists alike are bringing their children in increasing numbers to Hong Kong, and many deluxe and top-end hotels, including the Peninsula (p110), the Island Shangri-La and the Mandarin Oriental, have special programs for children, ranging from art workshops to Chinese cookery lessons.

Children are generally welcome in Hong Kong's restaurants – especially Chinese ones. Few restaurants have highchairs, however, so bring your own if you can't do without. Though most restaurants don't do special children's servings, Chinese food is generally shared and it's easy to create your own munchkin-sized portion.

Most hotels will be able to recommend babysitters if you have daytime appointments or are considering a night out without the kid(s). Otherwise contact **Rent-a-Mum** (☎ 2523 4868; www.rent-a-mum.com) and expect to pay $130 to $180 per hour.

BEST CHILDREN'S ATTRACTIONS
> Ngong Ping Skyrail (p143)
> Ocean Park (p102)
> The Peak (p74)
> Tsim Sha Tsui Promenade (p112)

BEST EDUCATIONAL FUN
> Hong Kong Maritime Museum (p102)
> Hong Kong Museum of History (p108)
> Hong Kong Space Museum (p109)
> Hong Kong Wetland Park (pictured right; p138)
> Hong Kong Zoological & Botanical Gardens (p44)

MACAU

Macau (p145) is a dichotomy. On the one hand, the fortresses, churches and food of its former colonial master, Portugal, speak to a uniquely Mediterranean style on the South China Coast. On the other, Macau is the now the self-styled Las Vegas of the East, which is why the vast majority of Chinese visit the place. But there's a lot more to Macau than just gambling (p152). The tiny peninsular and the islands of Coloane (p154) and Taipa (p154) constitute a colourful palette of pastels and ordered greenery.

The Portuguese influence is everywhere – cobbled back streets, baroque churches, ancient stone fortresses, art-deco apartment buildings, and restful parks and gardens – and there are several world-class museums. Having said that, it is worth making some time for a gawp at the casinos even if you're not here for the gambling. The buildings alone compete to outdazzle each other, while inside, the casino complexes offer an ever-more enticing mix of entertainment, including big-name musicians, its own Cirque du Soleil troupe, some excellent fine dining and lashings of opulence.

BEST SIGHTS
> Casinos (p152)
> Lou Lim loc Garden (p149)
> Macau Museum (p149)
> Ruins of the Church of St Paul (pictured above; p150)

BEST PORTUGUESE & MACANESE RESTAURANTS
> A Lorcha (p150)
> Clube Militar de Macau (p151)
> Fernando (p155)
> Restaurante Litoral (p151)

MUSEUMS & GALLERIES

Hong Kong boasts some two dozen museums scattered across the territory, exploring everything from tea ware (p80) and space exploration (p109) to horse racing (see the boxed text, p89) and the history of medicine (p76). Among the most worthwhile cultural experiences are the excellent Hong Kong Museum of History (p108) in Tsim Sha Tsui East, and the Hong Kong Heritage Museum (p138) in the New Territories, both of which do a fine job of explaining Hong Kong's history and culture. The Hong Kong Museum of Art (p108) offers a good introduction to Chinese fine and applied arts through its worthwhile temporary exhibitions and its diverse and dazzling permanent collection of painting, ceramics, calligraphy and antiquities. At the same time, Hong Kong counts twice as many galleries that show everything from cutting-edge home-grown art to old photographs and 'decorative' pieces created to 'blend in'. Some 40 galleries, both commercial and government-supported, take part in the annual Hong Kong Art Walk (p29) in March.

BEST FOR ART
> Hong Kong Museum of Art (pictured above; p108)
> Para/Site Art Space (p45)
> Shanghai St Artspace (p124)

BEST FOR CULTURE
> Hong Kong Heritage Museum (p138)
> Hong Kong Museum of History (p108)
> Law Uk Folk Museum (p96)

BEST FOR KIDS
> Hong Kong Maritime Museum (p102)
> Hong Kong Science Museum (p109)
> Hong Kong Space Museum & Space Theatre (p109)

BEST FOR CONTEMPORARY HONG KONG ART
> Grotto Fine Art (p58)
> Hanart TZ Gallery (p48)

PARKS & GARDENS

Hong Kong's precious green spaces are surprisingly profuse and varied. The territory counts almost two dozen country parks (mostly in the New Territories, p136, and the Outlying Islands, p140) where you can walk, hike, bird-watch etc. But you don't have to travel great distances in Hong Kong in order to commune with nature; the urban areas of Hong Kong Island and Kowloon are hardly devoid of parks and gardens. Some, such as Hong Kong Park (p80), are laid out to 'reflect' rather than 'represent' nature, and are awash in fake waterfalls and stone 'mountains', while others, such as Hong Kong Wetland Park (p138), embrace Mother Nature with open arms. As well as these managed havens, Hong Kong offers a wilder side. It's easy to imagine you've left the city behind at places like the Sai Kung Peninsula (p138). Relatively hard to get to and almost uninhabited, it offers great promise for hikers, beach bums and boat lovers alike. A more challenging way to experience these wilder open spaces is to tackle one of the great trails, such as the MacLehose Trail (p138), which traverses the New Territories, or the 78km Wilson Trail (p100), which snakes through Hong Kong Island's hilly, green backyard.

BEST FOR...
Wildlife Hong Kong Zoological & Botanical Gardens (p44) and Hong Kong Wetland Park (p138)
History along with the greenery Kowloon Walled City Park (pictured above; p132)
Museums Hong Kong Park (p80)
T'ai chi practice Victoria Park (p92)
Art Kowloon Park (p110)

SHOPPING

Hong Kong may not be the bargain basement it once was, but it still wins hands-down in the region for variety and competitive consumerism. Any international brand worthy of its logo sets up at least one shop here, and a handful of local brands are worth spending your money on. Clothing (ready made or tailored), shoes, jewellery, luggage and, to a lesser a degree nowadays, electronic goods are the city's strong suits.

There is no sales tax (for the moment at least), so the marked price is the price you'll pay. Credit cards are widely accepted, except in markets. It's rare for traders to accept travellers cheques or foreign currency as payment. Sales assistants in department or chain stores rarely have any leeway to give discounts, but you can try bargaining in owner-operated shops and certainly in markets.

You can count on shops in Central (p47) to be open from 10am to 6pm or 7.30pm daily. In Causeway Bay (pictured below; p93) and Wan Chai (p81) many will stay open until 9.30pm or 10pm. In Tsim Sha Tsui (p112), Yau Ma Tei (p125) and Mong Kok (p125) they close around 9pm.

BEST FOR PERIOD PIECES
> Amours Antiques (p57)
> Chine Gallery (p58)
> Hobbs & Bishops Fine Art (p58)
> Wattis Fine Art (p60)

BEST FOR FASHION
> Blanc de Chine (p48)
> Joyce (p49)
> Kent & Curwen (p82)

> Pacific Custom Tailors (p82)
> Vivienne Tam (p82)

BEST FOR GIFTS & SOUVENIRS
> Chinese Arts & Crafts (p113)
> Liuligongfang (p49)
> Shanghai Tang (p50)
> Yue Hwa Chinese Products Emporium (p127)

VEGETARIAN

Beware: there are a hundred ways to eat meat on the seemingly meat-free menu items in ordinary restaurants, meat-stock simmered vegetables being the most common problem. Stick to the specialists and you'll be fine.

Chinese vegetarian food has undergone a renaissance in recent years, and is consumed by devout Buddhists and the health conscious alike. Large monasteries in Hong Kong, including Po Lin Monastery (pictured below; p144) on Lantau, often have vegetarian restaurants, though you will also find many vegetarian restaurants in Kowloon and on Hong Kong Island. For the most part they are Cantonese or Shanghainese and strictly vegetarian as they are owned and operated by Buddhists.

Meatless dishes can be found elsewhere: vegetarian congee is available in most noodle shops, and dim sum houses serve a number of vegetarian treats, including *chongyau beng* (onion cakes) and *fu pei gun* (crispy tofu roll), but be cautious.

Western vegetarian food is less easy to come by if you want anything more complex than a salad, but there are a few options in Central (p51) and on Lamma Island (p143). Some Indian restaurants are exclusively vegetarian, but most in Hong Kong offer a combined menu.

BEST FOR...
Vegan food Life (p63)
Shanghainese vegetarian food Kung Tak Lam (p95)
Vegetarian brunch Bookworm Café (p143)

SNAPSHOTS

VIEWS

Nothing quite matches Hong Kong from above but, then, it's difficult to get things wrong with mountains on one side, water on the other and skyscrapers in the middle to provide the platform. And it's not just for thrill-seekers; fantastic views of the harbour form the backdrop of some excellent restaurants and a fair number of bars and clubs as well. Remember, too, that it's not just about Hong Kong from the top down. Some of the most dramatic sights in the territory are those of Hong Kong from the ground up. Just stand at the water's edge on the promenade in Tsim Sha Tsui (p112) and you'll understand. Views on the move are another good way to soak up Hong Kong's uniquely energetic vistas, whether it means boarding a Star Ferry (p10) or watching an urban panorama scroll by aboard a clanking, ancient tram (p13).

BEST VANTAGE POINTS
> Bank of China Tower Viewing Platform (p42)
> Hong Kong Monetary Authority Information Centre (p46)
> Ocean Park (pictured above; p102)
> The Peak (p74)
> Tsim Sha Tsui Promenade (p112)

BEST RESTAURANTS WITH A VIEW
> Aqua (p116)
> Felix (p117)
> Pearl on the Peak (p77)
> Petrus (p84)

BEST FOR A DRINK WITH VIEWS
> Aqua Spirit (p116)
> Lobby Lounge (p120)

Pay homage to the god of wealth in Repulse Bay (p102)

BACKGROUND

HISTORY

Until British marines clambered ashore to plant the Union Jack on Hong Kong Island in the early 19th century, this was a neglected corner of the Chinese empire inhabited by farmers, fishermen and, on 'remote' islands such as Cheung Chau (p142), pirates. Trade between China and Britain had commenced in around 1685, but the balance was unfavourable to the Europeans – until they began bringing opium into China in the late 18th century.

Despite bans issued by Chinese Emperor Jiaqing and his son and successor, Dao Guang, trade in opium continued until 1839 when the commissioner of Guangzhou, Lin Zexu, destroyed 20,000 chests – almost half a tonne – of the 'foreign mud' at Humen (Taiping). This gave Britain the pretext it needed to take military action against China. British gunboats besieged Guangzhou and then sailed north, forcing the Chinese to negotiate. Captain Charles Elliot, the chief superintendent of trade, demanded that a small, hilly island near the mouth of the Pearl River be ceded 'in perpetuity' to the English crown. Hong Kong formally became a British possession in August 1842.

The so-called Second Anglo-Chinese War (1856–60) won the Kowloon peninsula – and control of Victoria Harbour – for the British. Less than 40 years later, China agreed to lease the much larger 'New Territories' to Britain for a period of 99 years.

Steady numbers of Chinese refugees fleeing war and famine entered the colony from the early 20th century up to the late 1930s. In 1941 Japanese forces swept down from Guangzhou and occupied Hong Kong for four years, imprisoning both local Chinese and foreigners at Stanley Fort.

The communist revolution in China in 1949 sent more refugees pouring into Hong Kong. On a paltry, war-scarred foundation, local and foreign businesses built an immense manufacturing (notably textiles and garments) and financial services centre that transformed Hong Kong into one of the world's great economic successes. By 1960 Hong Kong was home to about 3 million people, up from a population of 600,000 at the end of WWII.

In 1967, at the height of the so-called Cultural Revolution in China, violent riots provoked by Mao Zedong's ultra-leftist Red Guards rocked the colony. Panic spread, but Hong Kong stood firm; Chinese Premier

CHINA'S INVASION PLAN

The peaceful agreement that eventually settled the status of Hong Kong after 1997 could have gone another way.

Margaret Thatcher, the British Prime Minister who negotiated the deal, said Deng Xiaoping, then China's leader, told her he 'could walk in and take the whole lot this afternoon.'

Lu Ping, the top Chinese negotiator, recently confirmed this was no bluff on Deng's part. Deng feared that announcing the date for the 1997 handover would provoke serious unrest in Hong Kong compelling China to invade.

Chou Enlai intervened and Hong Kong got on with the business it knew best: making money.

Few gave much thought to Hong Kong's future until the late 1970s, when the British and Chinese governments started meeting to decide what would happen in (and after) 1997. Though Britain was legally bound to hand back only the New Territories, and not Hong Kong Island and Kowloon, which had been ceded 'in perpetuity', most of the population lived there; it would have been an untenable division. In December 1984 Britain formally agreed to hand back the entire territory, and a joint declaration affirmed that the 'Hong Kong Special Administrative Region' would retain its social, economic and legal systems for 50 years after the handover.

Nervousness increased as the handover date drew closer, especially after 1989 when Chinese troops opened fire on and killed pro-democracy demonstrators in Beijing's Tiananmen Square, and both people and capital moved to safe havens overseas. A belated attempt by Britain to increase the number of democratically elected members of Hong Kong's Legislative Council spurred China to set up a pro-Beijing Provisional Legislative Council across the border in Shenzhen. On 1 July 1997 this body took office in Hong Kong, and Shanghai-born shipping magnate Tung Chee Hwa was named chief executive.

Hong Kong has weathered many storms in the decade since becoming a part of China again, including a severe economic downturn, several outbreaks of deadly Severe Acute Respiratory Syndrome (SARS) and the crucial intervention by Chinese authorities in what has been referred to as the 'upstairs demotion' of Tung, who had been returned for a second five-year term as chief executive in 2002.

Since 2002 Hong Kong has boomed again and with a slightly more popular chief executive, Sir Donald Tsang, the public mood has brightened of late.

> **HONG KONG IN PRINT**
> > *Hong Kong: Epilogue to an Empire* (Jan Morris) Anecdotal and very readable history of Hong Kong.
> > *Myself a Mandarin* (Austin Coates) Very charming and highly recommended memoir of a special magistrate in the New Territories of the 1950s.
> > *Old Hong Kong* (Formasia) If you like old pictures with your history, this three-volume work is for you.

GOVERNMENT & POLITICS

Hong Kong 'constitution' is the Basic Law, published in 1988, which in theory guarantees Hong Kong's freedom in everything except foreign affairs. Hong Kong's government is a complicated hybrid of a quasi-presidential system combined with a quasi-parliamentary model. An 800-member election committee chooses the chief executive, the leader of the executive branch of power, in an election that can go uncontested (and often does), giving rise to complaints by democracy advocates that the system does not represent the people.

The 60-seat Legislative Council considers and passes legislation proposed by the Executive Council. Half of its seats are returned by the voting public, the other half by occupationally based groups, or 'functional constituencies', groups the democracy campaigners accuse of being dominated by big business and of rendering the Legislative Council a mere rubber stamp for the executive.

The current chief executive, Donald Tsang, replaced Tung Chee Hwa in 2005. With the economy once again booming, and the withdrawal of Anson Chan, Hong Kong's most popular political figure, from the contest, Tsang was assured re-election in March 2007.

ECONOMY

Business is Hong Kong's heart and soul. The monopolies in certain sectors of the economy (eg transport and power generation) notwithstanding, the territory remains a capitalist's dream and the most economically free in the world, with trade virtually unrestricted, a hard-working labour force, excellent telecommunications and very low taxes (the maximum personal income tax is 16% while company profits tax is capped at 17.5%). However, the government is considering a general sales tax (VAT) to broaden the narrow tax base, something that would prove immensely controversial.

Service industries now employ about 84% of Hong Kong's workforce and make up 88% of its GDP; the manufacture of textiles, toys and other commodities now takes place over the border. Mainland China supplies almost 43% of Hong Kong's total imports and exports. Other important trading partners are Japan (12%), Taiwan (8%), the USA (7%), South Korea (5%) and Singapore (3%).

The start of the 21st century was a trying time for the Hong Kong economy. Hong Kong maintained an average GDP growth of 5% through the 1990s and peaked at 10% in 2000, but fell to just 0.6% in 2001. Three years later a surge in trade with China and a phenomenal increase of visitors from the mainland saw consumer prices rise (and deflation disappear) for the first time in almost six years. By 2007 GDP had reached US$42,000 per capita, unemployment was at a six-year low of 4.1% and real GDP growth had climbed back to 6.3%. Most importantly property prices, always viewed as a boom-or-bust gauge here, continued to soar (although thanks to convulsions in the global economy things looked less certain at the time of publication). If China continues to grow and Hong Kong with it (as looks likely), visitors should expect to see general prices rise over the next few years.

ENVIRONMENT

Pollution has been and remains a major problem in Hong Kong, but it wasn't until 1989, with the formation of the Environmental Protection Department (EPD; www.epd.gov.hk), that government authorities acted decisively to clean up the mess. The EPD has had to deal with decades of serious environmental abuse and – almost as serious – a great deal of public indifference about the implications of littering and pollution.

Hong Kong's waterways are in a terrible state, but there have been some slight improvements over the past decade. A disposal system in Victoria Harbour is now collecting up to 70% of the sewage, and the E. coli count indicating the presence of bacteria is improving. The quality of the water at Hong Kong's 43 gazetted beaches must be rated 'good' or 'fair' to allow public use.

Air pollution, responsible for an estimated 15,600 premature deaths a year, is an even more serious concern, especially now that it is hitting Hong Kong where it hurts the most: in its pockets. According to a survey

WHERE THE GRASS IS GREEN(ER)

Not all of Hong Kong is concrete and glass. Some 425 sq km – 38% of the total land area – has been designated as protected country parkland. These 23 parks and 15 'special areas' – for the most part in the New Territories and on the Outlying Islands, but also encompassing the slopes of Hong Kong Island – comprise uplands, woodlands, coastlines, marshes and all of Hong Kong's 17 freshwater reservoirs. In addition, there are four protected marine parks and one marine reserve.

conducted by the American Chamber of Commerce in August 2006, some 40% of senior executives polled said Hong Kong's worsening air quality made it difficult to recruit overseas staff. On the positive side, however, the governments of Hong Kong and Guangdong, where most of the air pollution originates, jointly committed themselves to reducing regional emissions of breathable suspended particulates, nitrogen oxides, sulphur dioxide and volatile organic compounds by more than half by 2010. An hourly update of Hong Kong's air pollution index can be found on the EPD's website.

SOCIETY & CULTURE

While Hong Kong may seem very Westernised on the surface, Chinese beliefs and traditions persist at every level of society. Buddhism and Taoism – mixed with elements of Confucianism, traditional ancestor worship and animism – are the dominant religions. In general, though, Chinese people are much less concerned with high-minded philosophies than they are with the pursuit of worldly success, the appeasement of spirits and predicting the future. Visits to temples are usually made to ask the gods favours for specific things, such as a loved one's health or the success of a business.

FENG SHUI

Literally 'wind water', feng shui (or geomancy) aims to balance the elements of nature to create a harmonious environment. It's been in practice since the 12th century, and it continues to influence the design of buildings, highways, parks, tunnels and other sites in Hong Kong. To guard against evil spirits, who can move only in straight lines, doors are often positioned at an angle. For similar reasons, beds cannot face doorways. Ideally, homes and businesses should have a view of calm water (even a fish tank helps). Corporate heads shouldn't have offices that face west: otherwise profits will go in the same direction as the setting sun.

FORTUNE TELLING

There are any number of props and implements that Chinese use to predict the future but the most common method of divination in Hong Kong are *chim* – the 'fortune sticks' (see boxed text, p133) found at Buddhist and Taoist temples.

NUMEROLOGY

In Cantonese the word for 'three' sounds similar to 'life', 'nine' like 'eternity' and the ever-popular number 'eight' like 'prosperity'. Lowest on the totem pole is 'four', which shares the same pronunciation with the word for 'death'. As a result the right (or wrong) number can make (or break) a business or relationship. The Bank of China Tower (p42) officially opened on 8 August 1988; August is always a busy month for weddings.

ZODIAC

The Chinese zodiac has 12 signs like the Western one, but their representations are all animals. Your sign is based on the year of your birth (according to the lunar calendar). Being born or married in a particular year is believed to determine one's fortune, so parents often plan for their children's sign. The year of the dragon sees the biggest jump in the birth rate, closely followed by the year of the tiger.

ARTS

The phrase 'cultural desert' can no longer be used for Hong Kong. There are philharmonic and Chinese orchestras, Chinese and modern dance troupes, a ballet company and several theatre companies. And the number of international arts festivals seems to grow each year.

CHINESE OPERA

Chinese opera, an unusual hybrid of song, dialogue, mime, acrobatics and dancing, is a world away from the Western variety and many foreigners find it hard to appreciate. Performances can last up to five or six hours, and the audience makes an evening of it – eating, chatting among themselves and playing musical chairs when bored, laughing at the funny parts, crying at the sad bits.

CATCH IT WHERE YOU CAN

The best time to see and hear Chinese opera is during the Hong Kong Arts Festival (p28) in February, and outdoor performances are staged in Victoria Park during the Mid-Autumn Festival (p30). At other times you might take your chances at catching a performance at the Temple St Night Market (p25) or Hong Kong City Hall (p53).

Costumes, props and body language reveal much of the meaning in Chinese opera – check out the enlightening display on Cantonese opera at the Hong Kong Heritage Museum (p138). For a better understanding of this art form join the Cantonese Opera Appreciation Class in the Hong Kong Tourism Board's 'Meet the People' program (see boxed text, p112).

CINEMA

While painting and literature enjoy a new lease of life in early 21st-century Hong Kong, the art of film-making remains largely moribund. Once the 'Hollywood of the Far East', churning out 245 films in 1994 alone and coming in third behind Hollywood and Mumbai, Hong Kong now produces only a few dozen films each year. What's more, up to half of all local films produced here go directly into video format, and are ultimately pirated and sold as DVDs in the markets of Mong Kok and Shenzhen. Imports now account for between 55% and 60% of the Hong Kong film market.

Modern Hong Kong cinema arrived with the films of Bruce Lee, who first appeared in *The Big Boss* (1971), and the emergence of kung fu as a film genre. The 'chop sockey' trend continued through the 1970s and into the early '80s, when bullet-riddled action films took over.

A new wave of more thoughtful, artistic films from directors in the late 1990s and early noughties made a modest name around the world for a less action-packed, more auteur driven Hong Kong cinema beside the usual martial-arts mayhem.

The annual Hong Kong International Film Festival (p29) in March, now in its third decade, is one of the world's major film festivals.

DANCE

Hong Kong's professional dance companies are the **Hong Kong Dance Company** (www.hkdance.com), for Chinese traditional and folk, and **City Contemporary Dance Company** (www.ccdc.com.hk) and the **Hong Kong Ballet** (www.hkballet.com), for classical and contemporary.

One traditional form of Chinese dance that lives on in Hong Kong is the lion dance. A dance troupe under an elaborately painted Chinese lion costume leaps around to the sound of clanging cymbals, giving the dancers a chance to demonstrate their acrobatic skills.

MUSIC

Classical music is alive and well in Hong Kong and very popular with local people. The city boasts Chinese, philharmonic and chamber orchestras as well as a sinfonietta. Established overseas performers frequently make it to Hong Kong, especially during February's Hong Kong Arts Festival (p28).

Hong Kong's home-grown popular music scene is known as Cantopop, a saccharine mix of romantic melodies and lyrics. Rarely radical, most of the songs invariably deal with such teenage concerns as unrequited love and loneliness. The music is slick and singable, thus the explosion of karaoke parlours. Veteran names in the music industry are thespian/crooner Andy Lau, Jackie Cheung, Faye Wong and Sally Yip. More recent arrivals include Leo Ku, Edmond Leung, Andy Hui and the female duo Twins.

PAINTING

Painting in Hong Kong falls into three broad categories: contemporary local, classical Chinese and classical Western. Contemporary local art differs from that of mainland China, as Hong Kong artists are largely the offspring of refugees and the products of a cultural fusion; they blend

HONG KONG ON FILM

> *Chungking Express* (1994) – Director Wong Kar Wai's portrait of two cops dealing with love and relationships. Powerful (and, at times, funny) stuff.
> *Infernal Affairs* (2002) – Andrew Lau and Alan Mak's star-studded, utterly gripping and multi-award winning thriller about a cop (Tony Leung) and a Triad member (Andy Lau) is way better than Scorsese's Oscar-winning remake *The Departed*.
> *In the Mood for Love* (2000) – Wong Kar Wai's stylish tale of infidelity and obsession stars Maggie Cheung and Tong Leung as two neighbours in 1960s Hong Kong who discover their spouses are having an affair.
> *Made in Hong Kong* (1997) – Fruit Chan's low budget award winner about a moody young gang member who finds the suicide note of a young girl is a bleak take on modern Hong Kong youth.

NO-NOS & DO-DOS

There aren't many unusual rules of etiquette to follow in Hong Kong; in general, common sense will take you as far as you'll need to go. But on matters of identity, appearance and gift giving, local people might see things a little differently than you do. For pointers on how to conduct yourself at the table, see the boxed text on p62.

> Clothing – Beyond the suited realm of business, smart casual dress is acceptable even at swish restaurants. On the beach topless is a local turn-off and nudity a no-no.

> Colours – These are often symbolic to Chinese people. Red symbolises good luck, virtue and wealth (though writing in red can convey anger or unfriendliness). White symbolises death, so avoid giving white flowers (except at funerals).

> Face – Think status and respect (both receiving and showing): keep your cool, be polite and order a glass of vintage Champagne at an expensive hotel. You've arrived.

> Gifts – If you want to give flowers, chocolates or wine to someone (a fine idea if invited to their home), they may appear reluctant for fear of seeming greedy, but insist and they'll give in and accept. Money enclosed in little red envelopes *(laisee)* is given at weddings and the lunar new year.

> Name Cards – Hong Kong is name-card crazy and in business circles they are a must. People simply won't take you seriously unless you have one (be sure to offer it with both hands). Bilingual cards can usually be printed within 24 hours; try printers along Man Wa Lane in Central (p40) or ask your hotel to direct you.

East and West and are concerned with finding their orientation in the metropolis through personal statement. The best places to see examples of this art are the Hong Kong Museum of Art (p108), Hanart TZ Gallery (p48) and Para/Site Art Space (p45).

THEATRE

Nearly all theatre in Hong Kong is Western in form and staged in Cantonese. Theatre groups include the **Hong Kong Repertory Theatre** (www.hkrep.com) and the more experimental **Chung Ying Theatre Company** (www.chungying.com).

DIRECTORY
TRANSPORT
ARRIVAL & DEPARTURE

Most international travellers arrive and depart via Hong Kong International Airport. Travellers to and from mainland China can use ferry, road or rail links to Guangdong and points beyond. Hong Kong is accessible from Macau via ferry or helicopter.

AIR

Sleek **Hong Kong International Airport** (Map p141, B2; ☎ 2181 0000; www .hkairport.com) is on Chek Lap Kok, an island flattened and extended by reclaimed land off the northern coast of Lantau. Highways, bridges (including the 2.2km-long Tsing Ma Bridge) and a fast train on 34km of track link the airport with Kowloon and Hong Kong Island.

The **Airport Express** (☎ 2881 8888; www.mtr.com.hk) departs from Hong Kong station ($100) in Central every 12 minutes from 5.50am to 12.48am daily, calling at Kowloon station ($90) in Jordan and at Tsing Yi island ($60) en route; the full trip takes 24 minutes. Vending machines dispense tickets at the airport and train stations en route. You can also use an Octopus card (p189). If you are booked on a scheduled flight and are taking the Airport Express to the airport, you can check in your bags and receive your boarding pass from one day to 90 minutes before your flight at Hong Kong or Kowloon Airport Express stations (open 5.30am to 12.30am).

There are also good bus links to/from the airport. Major hotel and guesthouse areas on Hong Kong Island are served by the A11 ($40) and A12 ($45) buses; the A21 ($33) does similar areas in Kowloon. Buses run every 10 to 30 minutes from about 6am to between midnight and 1am; the 'N' buses follow the same route after that. Buy your ticket at the booth near the airport bus stand.

OTHER WAYS TO GO

As noted in the introduction to this chapter, you don't have to take to the skies to reach Hong Kong – at least from the north (China) and the west (Macau). Travellers to/from mainland China make use of ferries, buses and trains. Indeed, the celebrated Trans-Mongolian and Trans-Manchurian trains will get you from Beijing to Moscow while very much on the ground; contact **Monkey Shrine** (www.monkeyshrine.com) or **Russia Experience** (www.trans-siberian .co.uk) for details. It's also possible to drive or take a bus to Macau and then catch a ferry to Hong Kong from there.

A taxi from the airport to Tsim Sha Tsui/Central costs around $270/340. **Parklane Limousine Service** (☎ 2261 0303; www.hongkonglimo.com) and **Trans-Island Limousine Service** (☎ 2261 2155; www.trans-island.com.hk) charge $450/550 to the same destination for up to four people.

TRAIN

Getting to/from Shenzhen over the border in mainland China is a breeze. Just board the **Mass Transit Railway** (MTR; ☎ 2881 8888; www.mtr .com.hk) East Rail (p186) at Hung Hom (Map p107, F1) or East Tsim Sha Tsui stations (Map p107, E3) and ride it for 40 minutes to Lo Wu (2nd/1st class $33/66); Shenzhen is a couple of hundred metres away.

The Kowloon–Guangzhou express train departs from the Hung Hom station a dozen times daily (from $190, 1¾ hours). Tickets can be booked in advance at MTR stations in Hung Hom, Kowloon Tong and Sha Tin; from China Travel Service (CTS) agents; or over the phone through the **Intercity Passenger Services Hotline** (☎ 2947 7888).

Another rail line links Kowloon with both Shanghai and Beijing. Trains to Beijing (hard/soft sleeper from $574/934, 24 hours) via Guangzhou, Changsha and Wuhan leave on alternate days. Trains to Shanghai ($508/825, 23 hours) via Guangzhou and Hangzhou leave on the other days.

BUS

Several transport companies in Hong Kong offer bus services to Guangzhou, Shenzhen airport and other destinations in the Pearl River Delta:

CTS Express Coach (☎ 2365 0118, 2261 2472; http://ctsbus.hkcts.com)

Gogobus (☎ 2375 0099, 2261 0886; www .gogobus.com)

Motor Transport Company of Guangdong & Hong Kong (☎ 2317 7900; www .gdhkmtc.com).

BOAT

Services to/from the Macau ferry terminal (Map p41, C1) run round-the-clock. Ferry tickets ($142 from Hong Kong Island; higher prices from about 6pm to 6am and on weekends) can be purchased at the terminals or by calling local carrier **Turbojet** (☎ 2859 3333; www .turbojet.com.hk). The **Cotai Jet** (☎ 2885 0595; www.cotaijet.com) departs from the Macau ferry terminal (economy/superclass Monday to Friday $134/236, Saturday and Sunday $146/52, night crossing $176/275) and connects with the new strip of casinos on Taipa Island in Macau.

Jet catamarans and hovercraft depart from the China ferry terminal (Map p107, B5) to destinations in Guangdong.

CLIMATE CHANGE & TRAVEL

Travel – especially air travel – is a significant contributor to global climate change. At Lonely Planet, we believe that all travellers have a responsibility to limit their personal impact. As a result, we have teamed with Rough Guides and other concerned industry partners to support Climate Care, which allows travellers to offset the greenhouse gases they are responsible for with contributions to energy-saving projects and other climate-friendly initiatives in the developing world. Lonely Planet offsets all staff and author travel.

For more information, turn to the responsible travel pages on www.lonelyplanet.com. For details on offsetting your carbon emissions and a carbon calculator, go to www.climatecare.org.

VISA

Visas are not required for citizens of the UK (up to 180 days), of other EU countries, Australia, Canada, Israel, Japan, New Zealand, the USA (90 days) and South Africa (30 days). Others should check visa regulations at www.immd.gov.hk before leaving home.

RETURN/ONWARD TICKET

Visitors requiring visas have to show that they have adequate funds for their stay (a credit card should do the trick) and that they hold an onward or return ticket.

DEPARTURE TAX

The Hong Kong airport departure tax ($120 for everyone over 12 years) is almost always included in the price of the air ticket.

GETTING AROUND

Hong Kong is small and crowded, and public transport is the only practical way to move people.

The ultramodern Mass Transit Railway (MTR; p186) subway is the quickest way to get to most urban destinations. The bus system is extensive and as efficient as the traffic allows, but it can be bewildering for short-term travellers. Ferries are fast and economical and throw in spectacular harbour views at no extra cost. Trams are really just for fun.

In this guide we include icons – MTR, bus, train/tram or ferry – to indicate the most practical and convenient form of transport for each listing.

In this book, the nearest metro, bus, train/tram or ferry route is noted after the Ⓜ , 🚌 , 🚆 or 🚢 in each listing. See also the transport map on the inside back cover.

TRAVEL PASSES

The **Octopus card** (☎ 2929 3399; www .octopuscards.com), a rechargeable 'smart card' valid on most forms of public transport in Hong Kong, costs $150. This includes a $50

Local Travel Box

	Central	Peak	Causeway Bay
Central	n/a	🚌 Peak, 10min	Ⓜ Island line, 6min
Peak	🚌 Peak, 10min	n/a	Ⓜ Island line, 6min & 🚌 Peak, 10min
Causeway Bay	Ⓜ Island line, 6min	Ⓜ Island line, 6min & 🚌 Peak, 10min	n/a
Tsim Sha Tsui	Ⓜ Tsuen Wan line, 5min	Ⓜ Tsuen Wan line 5min & Peak,	Ⓜ Island & Tsuen Wan lines, 8min
Sha Tin	Ⓜ Island line, 6min & 🚆 East Rail line, 16min	Ⓜ Island line, 6min, 🚆 East Rail line, 16min & 🚌 Peak, 10min	🚌 170, 50min
Lantau	🚢 Lantau, 31-48min	🚢 Lantau, 31-48min & 🚌 Peak, 10min	Ⓜ Island line, 8min & 🚢 Lantau, 31-48min

refundable deposit and $100 worth of travel. Octopus fares are 5% to 10% cheaper than ordinary ones on the MTR.

For shorter stays there's the new **Tourist MTR 1-Day Pass** ($50), valid on the MTR for 24 hours after the first use.

TRAIN
Mass Transit Railway
The **Mass Transit Railway** (MTR; ☎ 2881 8888; www.mtr.com.hk) is clean, fast and safe and transports around 2.4 million people daily. Tickets cost $4 to $26 ($3.80 to $23.10 if purchased with an Octopus card; see p185). Trains run every two to 10 minutes from around 6am to between 12.30am and 1am daily on eight lines including the

Airport Express line (p183). Ticket machines accept notes and coins and dispense change.

The longer distance MTR East Rail line, which runs from East Tsim Sha Tsui station to Lo Wu on the mainland border, and West Rail line, which links Nam Cheong station in Sham Shui Po (New Kowloon) with Tuen Mun in the New Territories, offer the fastest route to the New Territories. The 30-minute rides to Sheung Shui on the East Rail and Tuen Mun on the West Rail, for example, cost just $12.50 and $15 respectively.

BUS
Hong Kong's extensive bus system will take you just about anywhere in the territory. Most

Tsim Sha Tsui	Sha Tin	Lantau
M Tsuen Wan line, 5min	🚌 182, 1hr	🚢 Lantau, 31-48min
M Tsuen Wan line, 5min & 🚡 Peak, 10min	🚌 182, 1hr & 🚡 Peak, 10min	🚢 Lantau, 31-48min & 🚡 Peak, 10min
M Island & Tsuen Wan lines, 8min	🚌 170, 50min	M Island line, 8min & 🚢 Lantau, 31-48min
n/a	🚆 East Rail line, 16min & 🚢 Lantau, 31-48min, Sat & Sun 35min	M Tsuen Wan line, 5min
🚆 MTR East Rail, 16min	n/a	🚢 Lantau, 31-48min & 🚌 182, 1hr
M Tsuen Wan line, 5min & 🚢 Lantau, 31-48min, on weekends Lantau, 35min	🚢 Lantau, 31-48min, & 🚌 182, 1hr	n/a

buses run from 5.30am or 6am until midnight or 12.30am, though there are a handful of night buses that run from 12.45am to 5am or later. Bus fares cost $1.20 to $45, depending on the destination, with night buses costing $12.80 to $31. You will need exact change or an Octopus card (p185).

Central's most important terminal for buses is below Exchange Square (p42). From here you can catch buses to Aberdeen, Repulse Bay, Stanley and other destinations on the southern side of Hong Kong Island. In Kowloon the Star Ferry bus terminal (Map p107, B4) has buses heading up Nathan Rd and to the Hung Hom train station.

Figuring out which bus you want can be difficult, although it's useful to know that any bus number ending with the letter M (eg 40M) goes to an MTR station and that buses with an X are express ones.

MINIBUSES

Also known as 'public light buses' (an official term that no-one ever uses in conversation), minibuses seat up to 16. Small red 'minibuses' ($2 to $20) don't run regular routes; you can get on or off unless restricted by road rules. Green 'maxicabs' operate on some 350 set routes and make designated stops. Two popular routes are the 6 ($4.50) from Hankow Rd in Tsim Sha Tsui to

Tsim Sha Tsui East and Hung Hom station in Kowloon, and the 1 ($8) to Victoria Peak from next to Hong Kong station.

TRAM

Hong Kong Island's double-decker trams are not fast but are fun and cheap and a great way to explore the northern coast. For a flat fare of $2 (dropped in a box beside the driver as you disembark) you can rattle along as far as you like over 16km of track, 3km of which wends its way into Happy Valley. Trams operate from around 6am to as late as 12.30am and run every two to 10 minutes.

There are six routes (west to east): Kennedy Town–Western Market, Kennedy Town–Happy Valley, Kennedy Town–Causeway Bay, Sai Ying Pun (Whitty St)–North Point, Sheung Wan (Western Market)–Shau Kei Wan and Happy Valley–Shau Kei Wan. The longest run (Kennedy Town–Shau Kei Wan, with a change at Western Market) takes about 1½ hours. For more tram information, see p13.

Strictly speaking a funicular, the Peak Tram (one way/return adult $37/48, senior and child 3 to 11 years $16/23) departs for Victoria Peak about every 10 to 15 minutes from 7am to midnight. The tram's

NEED TO KNOW

Electricity The standard voltage is 220V, 50Hz AC. Most electric outlets are designed to accommodate the British variety with three square pins.

Metric System The metric system is officially used, but traditional Chinese weights and measures persist at local markets, including leung (37.8g) and gan (catty; about 605g). There are 16 leung to the gan.

Newspapers & Magazines The local English-language newspapers are the **South China Morning Post** (www.scmp.com) published daily ($7), and the **Hong Kong Standard** (www.thestandard.com.hk) Monday to Saturday ($6). The Beijing mouthpiece **China Daily** (www.chinadaily.com.cn) prints a Hong Kong English–language edition ($6). The *Asian Wall Street Journal* as well as regional editions of *USA Today*, the *International Herald Tribune* and the *Financial Times* are printed in Hong Kong.

Radio Popular English-language stations in Hong Kong are RTHK Radio 3 (current affairs and talkback; 567AM, 1584AM, 97.9FM and 106.8FM), RTHK Radio 4 (classical music; 97.6FM-98.9FM), RTHK Radio 6 (BBC World Service relays; 675AM), AM 864 (hit parade; 864AM) and Metro Plus (news; 1044AM).

Television The two English-language terrestrial stations are TVB Pearl and ATV World.

Time Hong Kong Standard Time is eight hours ahead of GMT; there is no daylight saving time in summer.

lower terminus (Map p41, E4; 33 Garden Rd, Central) is behind St John's Building, at the northwestern corner of Hong Kong Park. See also p18.

BOAT

There are four Star Ferry routes, but by far the most popular is the one running between its new home (Outlying Islands ferry terminal pier 7; Map p41, F1) in Central and Tsim Sha Tsui (Map p107, B4). Fares are $1.70/2.20 (lower/upper deck) and, quite frankly, there's no other trip like it in the world. Star Ferries also links Central with Hung Hom and Wan Chai with Hung Hom and Tsim Sha Tsui. For more on Star Ferries, see p10.

Two separate ferry companies operate services to the outlying islands, including Lantau, Cheung Chau and Lamma, from ferry terminal piers 4, 5 and 6 (Map p41, E1) in Central.

TAXI

Hong Kong taxis are a bargain compared to taxis in other world-class cities. The flag fall for taxis on Hong Kong Island and Kowloon is $16 for the first 2km and $1.40 for every additional 200m. It's slightly less in the New Territories ($13.50/1.20) and on Lantau ($12/1.20).

CAR & MOTORCYCLE

It would be sheer madness for a newcomer to consider driving in Hong Kong. Traffic is heavy, the roads can get hopelessly clogged, and finding a parking space is difficult and very expensive.

If you do need to use a vehicle, hire one with a driver from **Ace Hire Car** (☎ 2572 7663, 2893 0541; www.acehirecar.com.hk), which has chauffeur-driven cars for $160 to $250 per hour (minimum two to five hours, depending on location).

PRACTICALITIES
BUSINESS HOURS

Business hours are 9am to 5.30pm or 6pm Monday to Friday and (sometimes) 9am to noon or 1pm on Saturday. Many offices close for lunch between 1pm and 2pm.

Shops catering to the tourist trade keep longer hours, but almost nothing opens before 9am, and many shops don't open until 10am or even 10.30am. Even tourist-related businesses shut down by 10pm.

Most banks, post offices, shops and attractions are closed on public holidays. Restaurants usually open daily, including Sunday.

CLIMATE & WHEN TO GO

October, November and nearly all of December are the best months to visit. Temperatures are moderate in Hong Kong during these months, the skies are clear and the sun shines. January and February are cloudy and cold but dry. It's warmer from March to May but the humidity is high, with lots of fog and drizzle. The sweltering heat and humidity from June to September can make for some sweaty sightseeing; the threat of typhoon looms throughout September.

Travel in and out of Hong Kong can be especially difficult during Chinese New Year (late January/early February).

DISCOUNTS

Children aged three to 11 and seniors over 60 or 65 are generally offered half-price admission at attractions and on most forms of transport, but family tickets are rare.

The International Student Identity Card (ISIC) offers discounts on some forms of transport and cheaper admission to museums and other attractions. If you're under 26 but not a student, you can apply for an International Youth Travel Card (IYTC) issued by the Federation of International Youth Travel Organisations (FIYTO), which gives much the same discounts. Teachers can apply for the International Teacher Identity Card (ITIC).

EMERGENCIES

Hong Kong is generally very safe both night and day but, as with anywhere, things can go wrong.
Ambulance, Fire & Police ☎ 999
Police (crime hotline) ☎ 2527 7177
Rape Crisis Line ☎ 2375 5322

HOLIDAYS

New Year's Day 1 January
Chinese New Year Three days in late January/early February
Easter Four days in late March/April
Ching Ming Early April
Buddha's Birthday Late April/May
Labour Day 1 May
Dragon Boat Festival Late May/June
Hong Kong SAR Establishment Day 1 July
Mid-Autumn Festival Late September/October
China National Day 1 and 2 October
Cheung Yeung October
Christmas Day 25 December
Boxing Day 26 December

INTERNET

INTERNET CAFÉS

With the plethora of places offering low-cost or free wi-fi, including most hotels, all of Hong Kong International Airport (p183) and Cafe Deco (p76) on the Peak, you'll have no trouble accessing the internet with your own laptop. If you didn't bring yours along, Hong Kong has plenty of independent options:
Central Library (Map p91, D3; ☎ 3150 1234, 2921 0500; www.hkpl.gov.hk; 66

Causeway Rd, Causeway Bay; 10am-9pm Thu-Tue, 1-9pm Wed) Free access.

Pacific Coffee Company (Map p41, E1; ☎ 2868 5100; www.pacificcoffee.com; Shop 1022, 1st fl, IFC Mall, 8 Finance St, Central; 7am-11pm) Free access with purchase; one of scores of branches in Hong Kong, located within the Two International Finance Centre (p46).

Shadowman Cyber Cafe (Map p107, C3; ☎ 2366 5262; Ground fl, Karlock Bldg, 21A Ashley Rd, Tsim Sha Tsui; 8am-midnight Mon-Thu, 8am-1am Sat, 10am-midnight Sun) First 20 minutes free with purchase, then $10 every 15 minutes.

INTERNET RESOURCES

Lonely Planet (www.lonelyplanet.com) A good start for many of Hong Kong's more useful links.

Hong Kong Information Services Department (www.info.gov.hk)

Hong Kong News.Net (www.hongkongnews .net)

Hong Kong Observatory (www.weather .org.hk)

Hong Kong Outdoors (www.hkoutdoors .com)

Hong Kong Telephone Directory (www .pccw.com)

Hong Kong Tourism Board (www .discoverhongkong.com)

South China Morning Post (www.scmp .com.hk)

Time Out (www.timeout.com.hk)

LANGUAGE

Cantonese and English are Hong Kong's two official languages. While Cantonese is used in Hong Kong in everyday life by most (some 94%) of the population, English is still the primary language of commerce, banking, international trade and the higher courts.

However, there has been a dramatic rise in the number of Mandarin-speaking tourists since the handover, and some locals are now learning Mandarin in preference to English.

BASICS

Hello, how are you?	nei ho ma?
Goodbye.	baai baai/joi gin
I'm fine.	ngo gei ho
Excuse me.	m goi
Yes.	hai
No.	ng hai
Thank you very much.	do je saai/m goi saai
You're welcome.	m sai haak hei
Do you speak English?	nei sik m sik gong ying man a?
I don't understand.	ngo m ming
How much is this?	ni go gei do chin a?
That's too expensive!	taai gwai laa!

EATING & DRINKING

That was delicious!	jan ho mei!
I'm a vegetarian.	ngo hai sik jaai ge
The bill, please.	m goi maai daan

EMERGENCIES

I'm sick.	ngo yau beng
Help!	gau meng a!
Call the police!	giu ging chaat!
Call an ambulance!	giu gau seung che!
Call a doctor!	giu yi sang!

TIME & NUMBERS

today	gam yat
tomorrow	ting yat
yesterday	kam yat

0	ling
1	yat
2	yi (leung)
3	saam
4	sei
5	ng
6	luk
7	chat
8	baat
9	gau
10	sap
11	sap yat
12	sap yi
20	yi sap
21	yi sap yat
100	yat baak
101	yat baak ling yat
110	yat baak yat sap
120	yat baak yi sap
200	yi baak
1000	yat chin

MONEY

The local currency is the Hong Kong dollar (HK$). The dollar is divided into 100 cents. Notes are issued in denominations of $10, $20, $50, $100, $500 and $1000. There are coins of 10c, 20c, 50c, $1, $2, $5 and $10.

Hong Kong is a relatively pricey destination. You can survive on $300 a day, but it will require a good deal of self-discipline. Better to budget for around $600.

International travellers can withdraw funds from their home accounts using just about any of the numerous ATMs scattered around the territory. The most widely accepted credit cards in Hong Kong are Visa, MasterCard, American Express, Diners Club and JCB. For 24-hour card cancellations or assistance, try calling the following numbers:

American Express (☎ 2811 6122)
Diners Club (☎ 2860 1888)
MasterCard (☎ 800 966 677)
Visa (☎ 800 900 782)

For currency exchange rates, see the inside front cover of this book.

ORGANISED TOURS

There is a mind-boggling array of tours available via every conceivable conveyance. Some of the best tours are offered by the **Hong Kong Tourism Board** (HKTB; ☎ 2508 1234; www.discoverhongkong.com), and tours run by individual companies can usually be booked at any HKTB branch (p194). The more unusual tours include the Come Horseracing tour available through **Splendid Tours & Travel** (☎ 2316 2151; www.splendidtours.com) during the racing season. The tour includes admission to the Visitors' Box of the Hong Kong Jockey Club Members' Enclosures and buffet with drinks. Tours scheduled at night (Wednesday) last about 5½ hours, while daytime tours

(Saturday or Sunday) are about seven hours long.

As well as offering a scenic dolphin-spotting expedition, the four-hour tour (adult/child $360/180) off Lantau offered by **Hong Kong Dolphinwatch** (☎ 2984 1414; www.hkdolphinwatch.com; 15th fl, Middle Block, 1528A Star House, 3 Salisbury Rd, Tsim Sha Tsui) includes information on the plight of the endangered Chinese white dolphin, of which between 100 and 200 inhabit Hong Kong's coastal waters. Departures are at 8.30am from City Hall in Central and at 9am from the Kowloon Hotel in Tsim Sha Tsui every Wednesday, Friday and Sunday.

HKTB invites visitors on a free one-hour ride two days a week on a sailing junk called the *Duk Ling*. Boarding is at 2pm and 4pm on Thursday and 10am and noon on Saturday at the Tsim Sha Tsui public pier next to the Star Ferry terminal (Map p107, B4) in Tsim Sha Tsui. Visitors should register with any HKTB branch in advance.

If you're after faster, thrill-based water tours, the four-hour tour from **Kayak and Hike** (☎ 9300 5197; www.kayak-and-hike.com) of the harbour around Sai Kung in the New Territories takes you by unique 'fast pursuit craft' (FPC) to the otherwise inaccessible Bluff Island and the small fishing village of Leung

Shuen Wan. The tour price ($740) includes Chinese lunch as well as snorkelling gear. Tours depart from Sai Kung pier at 10am (9am on Sunday); book in advance.

Learn all about t'ai chi, feng shui and Chinese tea with a 4½-hour tour from **Sky Bird Travel** (☎ 2736 2282; www.skybird.com.hk). Tours depart at 7.30am from the Excelsior Hong Kong Hotel in Causeway Bay and at 7.45am from The Salisbury YMCA in Tsim Sha Tsui on Monday, Wednesday and Friday.

PHOTOGRAPHY & VIDEO

Any photographic accessory you could possibly need is available in Hong Kong. Stanley St (Map p41, D3) on Hong Kong Island is the place to look for reputable camera stores; Photo Scientific (p59) is especially recommended.

TELEPHONE

Hong Kong boasts the world's highest per-capita usage of mobile telephones, and they work everywhere – even in tunnels and the MTR. Any GSM-compatible phone can be used in Hong Kong.

Retail outlets **PCCW** (☎ 2888 2282; www.pccw.com) and **Hong Kong CSL** (☎ 2888 1010; www.hkcsl.com) rent and sell mobile phones, SIM cards and phone accessories. Handsets can be rented from $35 per day, and rechargeable SIM chips cost from

$180. Top-up cards come in $100, $200 and $500 amounts.

USEFUL PHONE NUMBERS

There is no Hong Kong area code.

Country Code ☎ 852
Local directory assistance ☎ 1081
International directory assistance ☎ 10015
International access code ☎ 001
Reverse-charge (collect) ☎ 10010
International credit card ☎ 10011
Time & air temperature ☎ 18501

TIPPING

Hong Kong is not a particularly tip-conscious place; taxi drivers only expect you to round up to the nearest dollar. Tip hotel staff $10 to $20, and if you make use of the porters at the airport, $2 to $5 a suitcase is expected. Most hotels and many restaurants add a 10% service charge to the bill (see boxed text, p65).

TOURIST INFORMATION

The very efficient and friendly **Hong Kong Tourism Board** (HKTB; www .discoverhongkong.com) produces reams of useful pamphlets and publications. Its website is also a good point of reference.

There are HKTB branches at **Hong Kong International Airport** (Map p141, B2; ☉ 7am-11pm), the **Star Ferry Concourse** (Map p107, B4; ☉ 8am-8pm) in Tsim Sha Tsui, and near Exit F of the **Causeway Bay MTR station** (Map p91, B3; ☉ 8am-8pm). Alternatively, call the **HKTB Visitor Hotline** (☎ 2508 1234; ☉ 8am-6pm).

TRAVELLERS WITH DISABILITIES

Disabled people will have to cope with MTR stairs as well as pedestrian overpasses, narrow footpaths and steep hills. People whose sight or hearing is impaired must be cautious of Hong Kong's demon drivers. On the other hand, some buses are now accessible by wheelchair, taxis are never hard to find and most buildings have lifts (many with Braille panels). Wheelchairs can negotiate the lower decks of most of the ferries, and almost all public toilets now have access for the disabled.

Contact the **Joint Council for the Physically and Mentally Disabled** (Map p79, C3; ☎ 2864 2931; Room 1204, 12th fl, Duke of Windsor Social Service Bldg, 15 Hennessy Rd, Wan Chai).

>INDEX

See also separate subindexes for See (p204), Shop (p205), Eat (p206), Drink (p207) and Play (p208).

INDEX

000 map pages

000 map pages

000 map pages

000 map pages